WORDS
OF
COMFORT
- Ray Comfort

Ray Comfort
Living Waters Publications
P.O. Box 1172
Bellflower
CA 90706

Printed in the United States

ISBN 1-878859-06-4
NKJV unless otherwise indicated
Cover -- Steve Hunt

First printing - September 1983
Second printing - November 1986
Third printing - August 1992

SPECIAL THANKS

My special thanks to my dear friend and cartoonist Richard Gunther. I want to take this opportunity to say that I don't know too many Christians who have both the love and dedication of Richard. Over the years he has done literally hundreds of illustrations for me. I have often been afraid I'd given him too much work, but a short time later the mail would bring, not only quality art work, but a letter from Richard saying " . . . more, more!" Such is his desire to serve God.

Although we are now living nearly 7,000 miles apart, I treasure fond memories of him preaching open air with a paper bag over his head, trying to illustrate the blindness of humanity (his personality comes out in his cartoons), and many other memories of praying and preaching together. Richard, may God bless you and your lovely wife Jenny and kids, and give you the desires of your heart.

DEDICATION:

This book is dedicated to my wife Sue, for her love, her faithfulness and for her help in making this book a reality; to my beautiful daughter Rachel for her many, many hours of typing and editorial help; to Dale Misclevitz and Christian Kingery for their assistance, and to my two boys Jacob and Daniel.

FOREWORD

It takes great discipline on my part to read a foreword, mainly because I have found by experience that the word "boreword" would have been more appropriate. So, if you are like me, I will endeavor to keep this one brief.

There seems to be a niceness but a uniformity about most devotional books. Usually they depict a sunset, an autumn leaf or such like. Obviously there is nothing at all wrong with them, but we trust that this one is just a little different both in cover and in content.

In this book you will find a menu of exhortation, edification and comfort, with just a dash of humor. It contains over 100 meals, each about 20 verses long (not too much -- Charles Spurgeon said, "I would rather lay my soul asoak in half a dozen verses all day, than rinse my hands in several chapters").

We hope that each day you will chew over these verses, meditate upon them, digest them and let them become part of you. Treat each day's reading as you would a meal. Wash your hands (Psalm 24:3-4), say grace (Psalm 119:18), then begin the main course (Jeremiah 15:16). After thoroughly chewing over the main course, partake of a few Words of Comfort for dessert, and then have a thought-provoking "Quote for Today" as an after-dinner mint to round off a satisfying meal.

May God bless you as you partake, and may your soul "delight itself in fatness" as you eat "that which is good."

MONDAY

READING: Revelation 3:14-20

MEMORY VERSE: "As many as I love, I rebuke and chasten. Therefore be zealous and repent." Revelation 3:19

My parents were overseas, and my job was to go around to their home and check that their dog was O.K. As I opened the gate, a small dog, starved of human fellowship greeted me as only a dog can. It twisted and turned, jumped and yelped with sheer joy at seeing me. This canine  desperately needed homosapiens. After the initial greeting, the animal ran off and eagerly returned with a ball in its mouth. With enthusiastic anticipation, it dropped the ball at my feet. I felt sad that I hadn't visited him sooner; so with great enthusiasm, I lifted my foot back and with a little extra vigor, kicked the ball to bring happiness to the little fellow. *Unfortunately, the dog was standing too close and I kicked it in the head.*

I wonder if you have ever wanted to bring happiness to someone, but you've actually ended up kicking him in the head. By that, I mean you've made a remark about someone's lack of height, their hairstyle, the size of their nose or some other physical feature, just for a bit of fun; but instead you have hurt that person and sent them away in pain. Perhaps the person may not even yelp, they just whimper and go away.

It is so easy to poke fun at someone, and even get a laugh from them and others; but it can be devastating.

I made a remark once about someone wearing white socks. Actually, my friend had white legs and I was making fun of them. It had always gotten a laugh before, but this time I really kicked the guy in the head.

It obviously hurt him. Perhaps he had been fighting self-consciousness about his "lily-whites," and it took all of his courage to wear shorts that day; and along comes ol' pea-brain Comfort and draws attention to them.

I was trying to make him laugh, but instead I brought him pain. I felt so bad about the incident, I asked him for forgiveness (and I also asked God to forgive me), and determined never again to poke fun at others. I hope God helps me on that one because it's so easy to do.

I think I know why there's such a problem -- the mouth is so close to the brain, there is too little time to stop thoughts getting past the lips. If the mouth was at the other end of the body, it would take longer to get thoughts to it, and maybe there would be time to stop something before it became words.

The design may have a social advantage but I'm sure it would lack a little visually.

QUOTE FOR TODAY: If you have an unpleasant neighbor, the odds are he has one too.

* * *

TUESDAY

READING: Revelation 4:1-11

MEMORY VERSE: "Holy, holy, holy, Lord God Almighty, Who was and is and is to come!" Revelation 4:8

I tried to organize a water baptism once with three local pastors -- Pastors Wade, Dunk and Bridges. I thought it would be unique to have an outdoor baptism with men with appropriate names. Unfortunately, the historical event didn't take place. Wade had a bad back and Bridges was out of town.

Our own church did have a baptism I wish I hadn't missed. They took a new convert down to the local beach and did the deed in the sea. It was a very memorable moment for the woman. A wave came as she went under and tossed her around somewhat. She went down smiling with joy and came up all gums -- *while under the water, her false teeth were knocked out and lost in the turmoil!* The newspapers carried the item and headed it up "JAWS." Somewhere there's a happy fish with a big grin. That incident bit a few hundred dollars out of the church budget.

If you haven't been water baptized, it's important that

you prayerfully study the Scriptures on the subject. I waited for two weeks before I went under the waters. No one told me about it until then, yet the Bible commands, "Repent and be baptized, every one of you in the name of Jesus Christ for the remission of sins." See that little phrase "every one of you." So you don't even need to pray about the subject.

The question may arise as to when, how, and who? For the "When?" take a look at the baptism of the Philippian jailer. He was baptized as soon as he was saved, in the middle of the night! The Ethiopian eunuch asked Philip, "What hinders me to be baptized?" Philip didn't say, "A six weeks training course." No, he just said that he may be baptized if he believed with all his heart; he did, and he was. For an answer to "How?" i.e. whether you should be sprinkled or dipped, check out John 3:23. John the Baptist was baptizing at a certain place "because there was much water there." If he was sprinkling, they would have only needed a cupful to do hundreds.

And lastly, "Who?" Who should you get to baptize you? It would be good if your pastor, or your minister would, but if that isn't possible, you can be baptized by any other believer. The Bible tells us that Jesus' disciples did the baptizing. I have heard of many people being baptized in their bath (clothed of course).

So what are you waiting for? Delight the heart of your Heavenly Father, follow the example of Jesus and pass through the waters of baptism. And by the way, if you have false teeth, keep your mouth closed.

QUOTE FOR TODAY:
"If I were God, and the world treated me as it treated Him,

I would kick the wretched thing to pieces." - Martin Luther

* * *

WEDNESDAY

READING: Joel 2:1-29

MEMORY VERSE: "And it shall come to pass afterward, that I will pour out my Spirit upon all flesh; and your sons and your daughters shall prophecy, and your old men shall dream dreams, your young men shall see visions." Joel 2:28

Most of us are familiar with the words of Scripture that tell us that life and death are in the power of the tongue. It's often brought to us with the admonition to keep our speech free from negative, deathly words of unbelief. But let's remember the positive aspect of that scripture -- we have the power of *life* in our tongue.

Before we go any further let me qualify myself. I'm not talking about the "name it, claim it" doctrine where you use the power that God has given to get things; where all I have to do is speak "Mercedes Benz" into the air and it will come to pass, if I believe.

What I am saying is that we have been given power through that which we speak.

When God brought creation into being, He didn't *think* "Let there be light," He *spoke* it. When Jesus brought Lazarus out of the grave, He didn't *think* "Lazarus come forth," He *spoke* it. Jesus said, "My words are spirit, they are life." In Hebrews 4, we are told that the Word of God is "living and powerful," and we are also told we have had "committed to us" the word of reconciliation. So, if you have a legitimate need (not a greed), don't just think your prayer, say it out loud. Use that which God has given you. Let the devil hear the Word, and show God that you really do have faith in His Word. Say, "God help me to rid myself of the fear of man. Spirit of fear I rebuke you in Jesus' name!" The Bible says, "The Lord is my helper, I will not fear what man shall do to me . . . I can do all things through Christ who strengthens me . . . if God be for us, who can be against us!"

There is another aspect of using the tongue God has given you to bring life. Use it to encourage others. We have so often used the tongue to bite and devour. Now that we love God, we must use that little unruly member to bring life to those who are around us. I was staggered some years ago when I called a Christian radio station, spoke to the D.J. and told him that I appreciated his ministry. It was the first time in two years that he had received a positive call!

When was the last time you said something encouraging to another person? How long since you called a loved one and said how much you appreciate them. Perhaps you do compliment pretty girls about how nice they look. Have you ever said a nice word to a "homely" girl. Pretty girls are always being complimented.

And while I am speaking in this line, let me practice what I preach. Thanks for reading this book. I mean it. I really appreciate that you have taken time out to listen to something I have to say . . . God bless you.

QUOTE FOR TODAY: Don't forget that appreciation is always appreciated.

* * *

THURSDAY

READING: Amos 8:1-14

MEMORY VERSE: "Behold, the days come, says the Lord God, that I will send a famine in the land, not a famine of bread, nor of thirst for water, but of hearing the words of the Lord." Amos 8:11

A friend related the following incident to me. During a spontaneous time of worship in a church, someone started singing, "He'll be coming round the mountain when He comes," supposedly referring to the Second Coming of Jesus Christ. The whole congregation joined in enthusiastically until they began the chorus, "Singing yi yi yippy yippy yi, singing yi . . . " after which they stopped and wondered *what on earth they were on about.*

A similar incident was told to me by a travelling Christian singer. He wanted to illustrate how much like sheep we are; how we follow each other without too much thought. He stated the following from the pulpit, "Things are more like they are now than they ever were before . . . Amen?" to which the whole congregation resounded with great fervor, "Amen!" They all agreed with something that didn't make an ounce of sense! The incident is rather amusing but it illustrates how easily led most of us are. We *are* like sheep.

I come from a country where there are plenty of sheep. In fact, New Zealand has just over three million people and over *seventy million sheep,* (they are not sure of the exact amount, because the guy who counts them keeps falling asleep). So I know quite a bit about sheep.

The first thing one should understand about them is that they are basically stupid. In my surfing days, as we were driving to the beach, if a sheep got on a dirt road in front of our car, it would literally run for miles in terror and never for one moment think of getting off the road. Man acts similarly as he runs from death, on the path of sin.

Or, if one sheep in a flock would jump in the air for no reason, the four or five following it would do the same. I have found the identical thing when I am giving out tracts to a crowd. If the first person takes one, the next four or five will. If one refuses, the next four or five will follow suit. The Bible tells us many times that we are like sheep. Wolves tend to wait for weak or lagging sheep that drop slightly behind the flock; we must not only make sure that we are moving with the mob, but that we also encourage others to keep on moving. But more than that, Jesus said to beware of "wolves in sheeps' clothing." So, each of us needs to keep awake and watch for those who would come into our midst, not only to pull wool over eyes and to fleece the sheep (which is bad enough), but also to devour, which is tragic.

QUOTE FOR TODAY: No matter what scales we use, we can never know the weight of another person's burdens.

* * *

FRIDAY

READING: Obadiah 1:1-21

MEMORY VERSE: "'Though you exalt yourself high as the eagle, and though you set your nest among the stars, from there I will bring you down,' says the Lord." Obadiah 1:4

Let me give you some details about the tragic life of J. Paul Getty. He was so rich, nobody knew exactly what he was worth. His money increased at such an amazing rate from so many different directions, it was incalculable. It was known that he did have an excess of a billion dollars in his piggy bank.

A photo I have of Mr Getty's face sums up his life. It is pitted with a sullen and grave bitterness. With all his wealth, it seems that Mr Getty had nothing to smile about. He had five marriages which fell apart. The youngest of his sons died at the age of twelve, his eldest died of an overdose of drugs and alcohol in mysterious circumstances, and his grandson was kidnapped.

Getty refused to pay the ransom because he suspected the whole thing was a hoax to get money from him. When the kidnappers cut off his grandson's ear, he decided it was time to do something about it. *He loaned the ransom money to his son at four percent interest!* His grandson was then released.

Meanwhile, one of his other sons became involved in the drug scene, and his daughter-in-law died of a heroin overdose. Then the kidnapped grandson, who was addicted to alcohol and drugs, had a stroke which left him permanently blind and paralyzed.

This called for daily, round-the-clock medical attention, which left him with a massive medical bill. His father, who had an annual income of twenty million dollars, refused to pay his own son's medical expenses and spent a fortune in court fighting a suit by his ex-wife. The whole thing confirms so graphically the many scriptures about the love of money -- "He that is greedy for gain troubles his own house" and "They that would be rich fall into temptation and a snare, and into many foolish and hurtful lusts, which drown men in destruction and perdition."

QUOTE FOR TODAY: "What greater rebellion, impiety, or insult to God can there be, than not to believe His promises." - Martin Luther

* * *

SATURDAY

READING: Jonah 1:1-17

MEMORY VERSE: "What do you mean, sleeper? Arise, call on your God; perhaps your God will consider us, so that we may not perish." Jonah 1:6

A young Christian mother once told me that she found motherhood unbearable. There was no other word for her 2 1/2 year old than "brat." She excused his behavior with the words, "He's such an active little fellow." But with a few carefully chosen words, I was able to convince her that her little fellow was actually an active little monster.

The good thing about the whole conversation was that this woman had had enough, to a point where she readily accepted what the Bible has to say on the matter. Scripture says that if you don't correct a child, (with a "rod," not the back of your hand), then you don't really love him.

Many mothers refrain from disciplining a child physically because they don't like the feeling they get when they do so. Yet, real love will correct a child when he goes off the straight and narrow. A true lover of a child will teach him respect for others and respect for all authority, so that when he grows up he will keep within the law.

The Houston Police Department prepared and published the following ten points called, "The Making of a Delinquent." It was distributed as a warning to parents who were indifferent to their child's welfare.

1/ Begin at infancy to give the child everything he wants. In this way he will grow up to believe that the world owes him a living.

2/ When he picks up bad words, laugh at him. That will make him think he's amusing.

3/ Never give him any spiritual training. Wait until he's twenty-one and let him decide for himself.

4/ Pick up everything he leaves lying about -- books, shoes, clothes; do everything for him so that he will be experienced at throwing all responsibility on others.

5/ Quarrel frequently in his presence. In this way he will not be shocked when the home is broken later.

6/ Give the child all the pocket money he wants. Never let him earn his own. Why should he have things as tough as you had them?

7/ Satisfy his every craving for food, drink and comfort. Denial may lead to harmful frustration.

8/ Take his side against the neighbors, teachers, policemen. They are all prejudice against your child.

9/ When he gets into serious trouble, apologize for

yourself by saying, "I could never do anything with him."
   10/ Prepare for a life of grief. You are bound to have it."

QUOTE FOR TODAY: "When we preach on Hell, we might at least do it with tears in our eyes." - D. L. Moody

* * *

SUNDAY

READING: Habakkuk 2:1-20

MEMORY VERSE: "For the earth shall be filled with the glory of the Lord, as the waters cover the sea." Habakkuk 2:14

Just near a place where I used to preach the Gospel on a regular basis, there was a group of alcoholics who sat each day on a church building's steps. The sight was a rather pathetic one, with their nicotine-stained fingers and filthy clothes. They would drink until they could drink no more, then sprawl out on the steps and sleep it off until they awoke and began the cycle all over again.

On one occasion, I had just finished preaching when one of the worst of them approached my car and tapped on the window for me to roll it down. Then this poor, bedraggled-looking man said, with a slurred voice, "You seen those punks . . . with their shaven heads . . . who'd like to be like one of them?" No doubt the shaven headed punks despised the drunks. I looked at both of them and said to myself, "There, but for the grace of God, go I," and no doubt both punks and drunks looked at me, and said the same thing.

Man has always had a distorted view of himself. The book of James speaks of man looking at himself in a mirror and immediately forgetting what sort of man he is. The Scriptures speak of us as being vainly puffed up, walking in the vanity of our minds. We are quick to see faults in others, but rarely in ourselves.

Instead of despising those around us and using them as some sort of ego-centric stepladder, we need to see ourselves as God sees us. That is one thought that is enough to sober me up into real thinking. I may fool friends and family, but I can never put on airs with God. One way to see yourself in truth is to turn to the love chapter in the Living Bible (1 Corinthians 13) and instead of reading the word "love," substitute your own name. I do it now and then and it has the effect of getting things into their right perspective. We used to use that chapter to discipline our children when they had fights. If they hadn't done anything bad enough to merit physical discipline, we would send them to their rooms and make them write out that chapter from the Living Bible two or three times, until they got the message. It is a message all of us need to be reminded of on a regular basis.

QUOTE FOR TODAY: "Nothing can make a man truly

great but by being truly good and partaking of God's holiness." - Matthew Henry

* * *

MONDAY

READING: Zephaniah 2:1-15

MEMORY VERSE: "Seek the Lord, all you meek of the earth." Zephaniah 2:3a

I couldn't help feeling sorry for one of our neighbors some years ago. He was one of those people who was easy to like. The poor guy spent a great deal of time and money pouring concrete, hour after hour, night after night, for a long driveway in the front of his new home. The finished article looked superb . . . until it rained. The water showed his errors. Puddles formed every two or three yards. So he took a sledge hammer and spent hour after hour, night after night, week after week, smashing it into small pieces, which he then loaded onto his trailer and took to the dump. Then night after night, etc. we heard the sound of a concrete mixer, mixing concrete as our likeable neighbor tried to rectify his mistake.

Finally, the job was completed. This driveway looked even better than the first. One could even say that it looked like it had been done by a professional . . . until it rained and revealed puddles slightly shallower than the first effort. He moved house.

A number of unlearned ungodly insist on saying that the Bible is full of mistakes. And they are right, it is full of

mistakes. It shows the mistakes of men (and women) on almost every page. Right from the beginning, the Scriptures show us the mistakes of others. The sin of Adam and the consequences that followed should be enough to put the fear of God in each of us.

Adam and Eve's sin was one of disobedience, and that human trait followed Israel right through until Pentecost, when God gave His Holy Spirit. Until then, men didn't have access to the "new heart."

Now each of us should be able to say, "I delight to do your will, O my God" because we have been born again. God has written His Law upon our hearts.

We are actually new creatures in Christ, with new desires. We look at all things in the light of God's will, in the light of His Lordship. We should be less prone to making mistakes because, not only do we have a new heart, but we also have the examples, both good and bad, of those who have gone before us.

QUOTE FOR TODAY: "It is through prayer and intercession that we administer the authority that is ours in the name of Jesus." - Derek Prince

* * *

TUESDAY

READING: Psalm 73:1-28

MEMORY VERSE: "My flesh and my heart fail; but God is the strength of my heart and my portion forever." Psalm 73:26

Every single day in the United States, millions of dollars are spent on physical fitness. There is actually a revival taking place, a revival fueled by fear of heart disease and other serious diseases.

In my teens I remained fit, at least from the waist up, through surfing. As married life came, and with it other responsibilities and priorities, my enthusiasm for fitness wasn't the only thing that began to sag. My male ego wouldn't call it fat, rather "loose muscle." So, one day, I actually went out and bought some running gear.

Each day for a week I can remember striding along the beach with the cool breeze on my face, the glistening sea beside me, the seagulls above, the warmth of God's sun on my back and thinking to myself, *"Oh how I hate this!"*

Too often I had seen the sorry sight of men in their mid-sixties doing their fitness bit. Their uniform was white running gear, red face, pained expression, often being pulled along at a slow running pace by an over-eager dog. Ironically, according to the experts, as they ran on the sidewalk, they were breathing massive amounts of car fumes and would do better for their health to stay at home. These are often the ones who enter the long distance "fun runs" and make it their last run. So whenever I ran, something would gnaw at my mind saying, "There must be an easier way!"

It happened while I was watching T.V. There, in full living color, was a man in his sixties actually smiling while riding an exercise bike. Before long, I had one by my bed. I couldn't manage a smile, but I did appreciate not having to run home when I got tired. I just jumped off the bike onto my bed. I managed to clock up about 60 miles . . . in just 210 days. When my father-in-law admired the bike, I felt an overwhelming urge to give it to him; so that's what I did!

A friend told me that five minutes skipping was equivalent to twenty minutes running. The thought of skipping exercise sounded like what I needed. Then I heard about a politician who died suddenly. The news item said that he was in "good health" at the time -- wonderful! Bet he flossed his teeth, took care of what he ate and kept himself fit.

So, now I do three minutes of exercise each day and that's all I'm going to do -- you won't get me carried away with workouts because we're all going to get *carried away* anyway. "For bodily exercise profits a little, but godliness is profitable for all things, having promise of life that now is and of that which is to come." 1 Timothy 4:8

QUOTE FOR TODAY: You know that you are unfit,

when you get puffed coming *down* an escalator.

* * *

WEDNESDAY

READING: Matthew 6:1-34

MEMORY VERSE: "When you pray, do not use vain repetitions as the heathen do. For they think they will be heard for their many words." Matthew 6:7

In our early years of marriage, Sue and I lived in a small wooden house not too far from the local voluntary fire brigade. Whenever there was a fire, an alarm sounded, calling the firemen from their jobs to action. The alarm was switched off from 11:00 pm to 7:00 am (thankfully).

It was during that period of time that an alarm sounded. The chief fire officer, who happened to be a friend of mine, told me the following story. The home alarms went off in the firemens' homes at about 5:00 am on a very cold, frosty winter's morning. An elderly woman, who lived in a two-story house down the street, had looked out of her kitchen window and seen smoke billowing from our roof. She called the station, and a dozen firemen jumped out of their warm beds and braved the freezing conditions.

After the fire truck silently moved along the road, it parked outside our house. It was then that the skillfully trained eyes of the firemen spotted steam, not smoke coming from our roof. Our hot water tank was overflowing through a pipe.

As the water hit the ice it sent steam into the air, giving the impression it was on fire. Knowing how I would feel, having to get out of a warm bed for mere steam, I'm sure a little heat was rising from the men as they drove back to the station. Without even being aware of it, we had caused a great deal of trouble.

Many a professing Christian also causes a great deal of trouble. These "spiritual butterflies" insist on fluttering from church to church, creating discord, full of unbelief and wanting counsel wherever they go. They are tools of the enemy sent to wear down the saints, leaving many a house of God steaming in frustration when instead, the Church should be burning with the pure fires of revival.

QUOTE FOR TODAY: "Ask not what God can do for you, but what you can do for God." - Darren Dreiling

* * *

THURSDAY

READING: Revelation 7:1-17

MEMORY VERSE: " . . . And God will wipe away every tear from their eyes." Revelation 7:17

I'm not the best of handymen. In fact, I am very dangerous with a hammer or a saw in my hand. Even with a paintbrush I tend to get more paint on Sue than I do on that which I am painting.

A friend once asked me to help him do some work on his boat. When the day was finished, he vowed never to let me near his boat again -- everything went wrong. I, however, was able to talk him into helping me repair a wall on the side of our house.

He showed up exactly on time at 8:00 am on the Saturday morning. I rushed to the door, opened it, trod on my shoelace and fell flat on my face at his feet. That day I only smashed one window. From then on, my friend would regularly come around to my business. At that time I made leather and suede coats to order. He would stand wide-eyed beside me, staring at my work, and saying he was witnessing a miracle, knowing how accident prone I was.

Rarely have I ever finished a handyman job without spilling some blood. When I was on the roof of our bird aviary, it collapsed. I lay on the ground in great pain for at least five minutes, laughing.

When I sawed through a thick piece of wood, which was too high for me to see the other side, I just about died of fright when I heard a loud bang. *I had sawed right through a live wire on the other side of the wood.*

I once finished a paint job without getting one drop of paint on my clothing or hands. I was so delighted, I put the lid onto the can and hit it with a hammer with even more enthusiasm than usual. The rim was full of paint, and consequently so was I.

When I was helping a lady put in an air conditioning unit, I stood on the outside of the window and she was on the inside. As I worked, I casually said, "You're a brave lady. My wife wouldn't stand that close when I am working . . ." Just then the window, unaided by human hand came down, heading for my fingers. Thankfully, the lady was able to stop it before it did any damage to me.

Maybe you're not exactly a brain surgeon. Maybe you too, make a mess of much that you put your hand to. You're not alone.

Not only do you have me to console you, but multitudes of others; one being the Apostle Peter. He sank when he stepped out of the boat, *but he did something the other disciples didn't . . . he walked on water!*

The fact is, it is not uncommon for me to mess up something I put my hand to. So what! If I gave up when I failed, I would never do anything.

When Solomon said to do what ever you do, with all your heart, he didn't speak of success, he just spoke of doing your best . . . and that's all God requires of those that love Him.

QUOTE FOR TODAY: When one will not, two cannot quarrel.

* * *

FRIDAY

READING: Revelation 8:1-13

MEMORY VERSE: " . . . the smoke of the incense, with the prayers of the saints, ascended before God from the angel's hand." Revelation 8:4

It's taken me quite some time to figure it out, but I have a quick metabolism. By that, I mean that I turn food into energy in about 2-3 hours. If I fast breakfast, I feel weak all morning (or should I say if I don't break my fast, I feel like mourning all week). If I eat food at 10:00 pm, especially food that contains sugar or protein, I wake up around 12:30 pm filled with energy, and have to burn it off with some exercise.

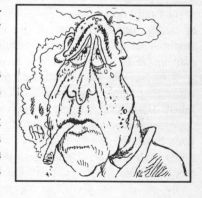

At our home in California we have a very large avocado tree. Almost all year round, spherical black gifts drop from Heaven and lie around our yard. Most mornings we pick them up and put them in a pile, then give them away. When I gave a friend a bagful he said, "Don't you like avoca-does?" I said I did, but they were too fattening. He said, "You're not fat." That's when I said, *"That's because I don't eat avocados!"* Actually the whole conversation started sounding a little like an Abbot and Costello skit.

His next remark was, "I thought you kept trim because you ran up stairs." I told him I only ran because I am impatient and that I have always run up stairs. He asked if I did a bit of running. So I said, "I hate running. In fact, I hate walking even more; that's why I run!" Actually, I am *longing* for my glorified body; a body that will never sweat, a body that doesn't get fat or tired.

The Bible is food for the soul. There are certain portions that act very much like sugar and protein. Those who don't feed on the Word regularly are as senseless as the person (and there are many), who slop down a cup of coffee each morning thinking that it will give their body energy for the day. Often a cigarette is smoked at the same time to keep the machine moving. That's like taking the cap off the gas tank, letting a bit of rain and smog filter in, and thinking your car will run fine.

One protein portion of Scripture that sends energy running into my soul, is the whole narrative of David and the big G. Have you ever wondered why he *ran* at Goliath? I think it tells us something about David's character. I would far rather run towards a problem than have it come to me. If you have some Goliath you have to face, ask the Lord to grab your hand and run towards it if you can. Get it over with.

Have you ever wondered why David took *five* stones in his hand? Maybe it was that Goliath had four big brothers, or maybe David wasn't 100% sure God would guide the first stone. If that's the case, it shows me he had more courage than if God had spoken to him, saying He would lay the rock in his forehead with the first sling. Just talking about the whole thing has given me energy. I hope it's done the same for you. I hope you need to go do a workout for the Lord.

QUOTE FOR TODAY: "In my experience, the best creative work is never done when one is unhappy." - Albert Einstein

* * *

SATURDAY

READING: Psalm 74:1-23

MEMORY VERSE: "You have set all the borders of the earth; You have made summer and winter." Psalm 74:17

I read once that there was a high survival rate for those attempting suicide by jumping off the Brooklyn harbor bridge. So there's a bit of good news for those would-be suicidees who don't really want to succeed. Bad news, however, for those who jump and do. A study by two doctors, whose hospital overlooked the bridge, revealed that the success rate actually depended upon the angle, the spin, and the date of fall . . . which determined the water temperature. Despite the bad news, the jumps are likely to continue.

"Suicide," according to the dictionary, is "the act of wilfully causing one's own death to escape a condition of living that one esteems intolerable." Of late, suicide has become a popular means of departure of this life.

Well, what causes ones to "self destruct?" There are many obvious reasons, such as overwhelming pain, guilt, self-hatred, debt, purposelessness or maybe a combination of each, just to name a few. Then there are those who commit suicide to escape the pain of old age. This was something a friend and I planned to do when we were in our mid-fifties. We supposed that as we aged and everything sagged and dropped off, so would the will to live, that death would just be a natural thing to glide into. Not so. Life becomes more valuable as time slips by.

Is suicide morally justifiable? Surprisingly, the Bible is silent on that subject, so I think that those whose religious organizations say they represent God on earth, are unwise when they maintain that those who take their own lives automatically go to Hell.

The subject is not so cut and dry as they would seem to suggest. God is the ultimate judge of the actions of humanity.

I dare not pass judgment on someone who was in agonizing pain, to a point where they took their own life; or the soldier who took his life by cyanide to escape horrific torture.

When I hear of someone taking their life because of depression or financial troubles, I feel grieved that those of us still living didn't somehow detect the symptoms, and reach out in compassion to the person involved.

May God give us tender, sensitive and loving hearts, to

perceive the states of mind of those around us who may be contemplating suicide to "escape a condition of living they esteem intolerable."

QUOTE FOR TODAY: "A belief that costs nothing and demands nothing is worth nothing." Jason Stellman

* * *

SUNDAY

READING: Psalm 75 & 76

MEMORY VERSE: "You, Yourself are to be feared; and who may stand in Your presence when once You are angry?" Psalm 76:7

I guess even Christians are in danger of becoming hardened by the increase of violence in society. Most people were shocked when they heard about a gang rape of an 8 month pregnant woman. The rapists held a leather jacket over her head while members performed "indecencies" and kicked her about the head. These types of incidents are becoming more and more common as pornography is produced en mass, not only in print, but on video.

One "expert" was given widespread publicity when he said, "No research ever has or ever will prove a casual link between pornography and rape." God knows his motive for such a statement.

In contrast, I was very moved by a talk back show on the subject of rape, where a woman spoke of her mother being raped and shared the consequences of the incident.

Her mother was so shattered that she had to go and live in another city with a group of elderly people for community protection. What moved me was the fact that the host began to speak frankly about the potential evil of his own heart. Such honesty makes one very vulnerable. I can't speak for all  males, but I know that most of us don't have to dig very deep to find dirt.

Many are calling for courts to deal out longer sentences for rape. Obviously this is only partly the answer.

It would seem that prison sentences, no matter how long, do little to deter "spur of the moment rapists" and provide little consolation for the women who have been violated. The gang who mass raped and beat the woman, actually threatened to kill their victim if she "spilled the beans," reminding us that this is often the case; and what we hear of in regard to rapes is only the tip of the iceberg. God only knows the terrible things which go on unnoticed by most of us.

QUOTE FOR TODAY: "Laughter is to life, what salt is to the egg." - Helen Valentine

* * *

MONDAY

READING: 1 Corinthians 3:1-23

MEMORY VERSE: "For no other foundation can anyone lay than that which is laid, which is Jesus Christ." 1 Corinthians 3:11

The Bible tells us of many a man's attitude to the problem of sin, but let's take a close look at three men who dealt with sin in their own way. Firstly, King Herod, a man full of contradictions. The Scriptures tell us that he feared John the Baptist; he listened to him regularly, yet he persisted in an open, adulterous relationship with his own brother's wife. John the Baptist must have been a thorn in the very side of the King's conscience, yet that so-called King had such a twisted sense of right and wrong, he had John beheaded so as to keep a promise. Perhaps Herod's wife felt that she had dealt with the problem once and for all; but John wasn't Herod's accuser, it was the Law of God . . . "You shall not commit adultery."

Another man of authority who dealt with the problem of sin was Felix, the Governor. When the Apostle Paul reasoned with him of righteousness, temperance and judgment, "Felix trembled." His guilt welled up within him and actually caused him to physically tremble as he saw the standard with which God will judge on that "great and terrible Day." Instead of yielding to the gentle wooing of the Holy Spirit, this procrastinator despised the riches of God's goodness and hardened his impenitent heart. Then, like so many, this "lover of darkness" had the gall to say to Paul, "Go your way for this time; when I have convenient season, I will call for you." I wonder if God gave Felix that "convenient season," or did He allow the angel of death to swallow him in his sins.

Then there was Festus, the new governor of Caesarea. After Festus heard Paul give his Damascus Road testimony, he cried out with a loud voice, "Paul, you are beside yourself; much learning has made you mad." Festus, as so many do today, wrote off the Gospel as folly, and God's servants as fools. The Jews said the same thing of Jesus -- "And many of them said, He has a demon, and is mad; why hear Him?" To those who are hardened by the "deceitfulness of sin," those in arrogance and pride, the Gospel is foolishness, but to us who are saved by it, it is the power of God. It is God's way of entry into everlasting life. Those who sit in darkness, in the shadow of death, under the wrath of the Law of God are in no place to bargain, argue or procrastinate but need to take heed in utmost sobriety the admonition of Scripture: "Today, if you hear His voice, harden not your heart."

QUOTE FOR TODAY: "Jesus has many who love His Kingdom in Heaven, but few who bear His cross." - Thomas A'Kempis

* * *

TUESDAY

READING: Malachi 3:1-18

MEMORY VERSE: "Bring all the tithes into the store-house, that there may be food in My house, and prove Me now in this, says the Lord of Hosts, if I will not open for you the windows of Heaven and pour out for you such a blessing that there will not be room enough to receive it." Malachi 4:10

Christian musician Keith Green released a very powerful, sobering song called "O God our Lord" in which he sang, "Who You gonna throw in the Lake of Fire, O God our Lord; the devil and the man with the dark desire, O God our Lord." When I heard it for the first time, I was a little taken back that anyone would want to sing about something so horrible; yet the song isn't to bless, but to motivate us.

Think on it for a moment; the Bible warns -- "Whosoever was not found in the Book of Life was cast into the Lake of Fire." It is truly a fearful thing to fall into the Hands of the Living God. We need to embark upon *desperate* evangelism, driven by the words of Paul,

"Wherefore knowing the terror of the Lord, we persuade men."

When I attended high school, we had a music teacher who was a little deaf. Sadly, we took advantage of this when he had his back to us while playing the piano. During a "free for all," I noticed that someone was being pulled by his leg under a seat two rows in front of me. So I crawled under the seats and grabbed the culprit.

As I did so, someone with a firm grip grabbed my leg and began pulling. I shook loose and kicked back with my foot. Then I turned my head around and saw that *it was the Principal who had stepped into the room to see what all the noise was about!*

I will never forget the feeling I had as the three of us waited in his office. The discipline came in the form of a rod being swiftly laid across the area designed for such a purpose.

The reason I felt so fearful was because of my guilt, and I knew I had punishment coming. How much more fearful will it be for those who stand before Him "from whom the heaven and earth flee" on Judgment Day! Pray that God gives you a vision of the awesome Day, then pray that God's love for sinners breaks your heart so that you will warn them to flee from the wrath to come.

QUOTE FOR TODAY: "Humility is pure honesty." - Jack McAlister

* * *

WEDNESDAY

READING: Luke 14:1-27

MEMORY VERSE: "Whosoever does not bear his cross and come after Me cannot be My disciple." Luke 14:27

Look at this Scripture: "If any man come to Me, and

hate not his father, and mother, and wife, and children, and brethren, and sisters, yes, and his own life also, he cannot be My disciple" (Luke 14:26). The first, second and third time I read that verse, I was shocked. Is this a mistranslation? Did Jesus really say to hate your mother, father, sister, wife, children, and even your own life? Doesn't the Bible say, "Husbands love your wives, honor your father and mother," etc? In fact, the verse is a real test of faith and humility for every Christian who seeks to understand God's will and Word. Do we have the humble obedience to trust Jesus and the Word with such a "hard saying?"

The answer to such a mysterious scripture is a simple one -- this is only one of the numerous statements of Jesus which can be classified as "hyperbole" or statements of extremity. Jesus often took opposites like love and hate, and put them together for contrast. He told the Pharisees that they "strained the gnat and swallowed a camel." He spoke of a camel going through the eye of a needle, and having a "log" in your eye. Scripture is consistent with such extreme statements -- for instance, "He that spares the rod, hates his son" (Proverbs 3:24). Obviously, many people love their children yet don't use the rod. The Bible is just emphasizing the importance of lovingly correcting your children with a rod or a stick, and not the back of your hand.

When Jesus spoke to the crowds in Luke 14:26, He was not bringing in a new ordinance, but as usual, He was reaffirming Old Testament scriptures. In Deuteronomy 13:6-9 we read, "If your brother, the son of your mother, your son or your daughter, the wife of your bosom, or your friend who is as your own soul, secretly entices you, saying, 'Let us go and serve other gods,' which you have not known, neither you nor your fathers . . . you shall surely kill him; your hand shall be first against him, to put him to death, and afterward the hand of all the people." Kind of sobering.

QUOTE FOR TODAY: "Every story of a conversion is the story of a blessed defeat." - C.S. Lewis

* * *

THURSDAY

READING: Isaiah 55:1-13

MEMORY VERSE: "For My thoughts are not your thoughts, neither are your ways My ways, says the Lord." Isaiah 55:8

"International Flavors and Fragrances" is a highly secretive New York based firm which specializes in artificially creating new and exotic fragrances and flavors. Using highly complex equipment, their flavor chemists break smells and tastes down to their component chemicals and recreate them synthetically.

They have produced the smell of salt air in cans labeled "The Ocean" for a museum in Florida. A restauranteur in California had them produce a smell of baked ham and Dutch apple, which he now sprays from aerosol cans to make his customers drool and the restaurant more enticing. What he is wanting to do is to create "desire" in their hearts, which will eventually find its way into their pockets.

When Jesus said, "You are the salt of the earth," He meant it. Not only does salt have properties of cleansing, preserving and flavoring, but it has the ability to create desire. We should be so salty that the world should desire the Water of Life. Jesus left us an example of how to create desire, not only in His lifestyle, but also in His words. Remember how His words created desire in the heart of the woman of Samaria? -- "Sir, give me this water that I thirst not, neither come here to draw."

Unregenerate humanity has no thirst for God. I wonder how many of them around us are beginning to desire to know Him because of our salty influence? Do they see our love, our peace in trial, our holy living, etc?

It would seem that a prerequisite for coming to God is desire. Isaiah says, "Ho, everyone that thirsts, come to the water." Jesus said, "If any man thirsts, let him come to Me and drink." The Holy Spirit says, "And him that is athirst come. And whosoever will, let him take of the water of life freely."

QUOTE FOR TODAY: "Collapse in the Christian life is seldom a blowout; it is usually a slow leak." - Paul E. Little.

* * *

FRIDAY

READING: Matthew 5:1-20

MEMORY VERSE: "Blessed are they who do hunger and thirst after righteousness; for they shall be filled." Matthew 5:6

It seems inflation has put a stop to the old English tradition of putting small coins into Christmas puddings. It's hardly worth a broken tooth for ten cents, and a dollar bill would be a little messy. But just as those of us old enough to remember enthusiasticly searching for those coins, so we should search the Scriptures for gems, with a similar attitude. Let's prod the following scripture with our fork: "And seeing the multitudes, He went up into a mountain: and when He was seated, His disciples came to Him. And He opened His mouth and taught them saying . . ." What does it mean "And seeing the multitudes"? Jesus had a

compassion for people -- He cared for the individual. When Jesus saw a sea of humanity, He ministered to them as He (humanly) could. By that, I mean He was limited by His human body. Having given His Holy Spirit, He can enter the multitudes individually, and actually "make His abode" within each believer, satisfying the hungry soul.

"And when He was seated . . . " This speaks of an intimate time with the Lord. He was going to stay a while and share His heart with them, thus His disciples came to Him. There is no point in coming to Jesus unless you are a disciple, i.e. someone who is disciplined to His Word.

"And He opened His mouth and taught them saying . . . " The unlearned may be tempted to ask the question, "How could He teach them anything without opening His mouth?" Jesus said and taught many things without opening His mouth. His lifestyle, His compassion, His love, His healing touch, His supreme sacrifice teaches us more today than the combined words of every teacher who has ever lived.

Let's not only learn from His example, but also learn to open up the Scriptures and find those precious coins of God's truth.

QUOTE FOR TODAY: "Whitewashing the pump won't

make the water pure." - Dwight. L. Moody

* * *

SATURDAY

READING: Psalm 149:1-9

MEMORY VERSE: "Delight yourself also in the Lord and He shall give you the desires of your heart." Psalm 37:4

To many people, a 'saint' is a holy person who lived centuries ago, usually depicted in paintings with a ring above the head, and a number of fat, winged babies flying about shoulder height. But those who believe the Bible know that you don't have to be dead for three hundred years to be a saint. In fact, the moment you repent and put your trust in Jesus Christ as Lord and Savior, God makes you a saint. By His grace,  through the medium of faith, God makes the sinner clean. He gives the believer a robe of righteousness, making him (or her) "unblamable in holiness" (1 Thessalonians 3:13).

One Bible commentator says, "In the New Testament the word "saint" always refers to a sanctified person, one set apart to God inviolably for His possession and service . . . all believers are saints regardless of their progress in experience and growth."

The Apostle Paul addresses his letter to the "saints who are at Ephesus," to "all saints at Colosse." To consider Christians as anything less than saints, is to undermine the redemptive work of Calvary. To see ourselves as sanctified saints is to merely see ourselves as we really are in Christ.

The honor of being called saints isn't just confined to the New Testament. Psalm 16:3 refers to us being His saints and encourages us to "sing to the Lord."

Psalm 37:28 says that God will not forsake His saints, while Psalm 97:10 says the Lord will preserve the souls of His saints.

When a Christian dies, Psalm 116:15 gives us tremendous consolation with the words, "Precious in the sight of the Lord is the death of His saints."

In Psalm 132:9 His saints are exhorted to "shout for joy," and in Psalm 149 "Let the saints be joyful in glory: let them sing aloud upon their beds. Let the high praises of God be in their mouth." Amen.

QUOTE FOR TODAY: "Fortify yourself with contentment, for this is an impregnable fortress." - Epictetus

* * *

SUNDAY

READING: John 14:1-26

MEMORY VERSE: "I am the way, the truth, and the life,

no one comes to the Father except through me." John 14:6

How sad it is that so few know who Jesus Christ really is. Many acknowledge Him as being a great teacher or a great philosopher, but the truth is, what we do with Him will determine our eternal destiny. He alone is the only way to God. He is the center-point of all Scripture, He is the very source of life itself.

Jesus Christ was Divine. There has never been another person like Him. When He passed through the waters of baptism, the Father spoke from Heaven, affirming His Divinity.

Demons have no doubts about who Jesus Christ is, " . . . and unclean spirits, when they saw Him, fell down before Him and cried, saying, You are the Son of God." In fact, their acknowledgment of His power is so real, the Bible says they tremble in fear.

Simon Peter, with all his glaring faults, knew who Jesus was. Jesus asked, "Who do men say that I, the Son of man, am?" When the disciples answered Him, He personalized the question with, "But who do you say that I am?" and Simon Peter answered and said, "You are the Christ, the Son of the Living God." Jesus emphasized personal confession of Him as Lord. The Scriptures say, "If you confess with your mouth the Lord Jesus . . . you shall be saved."

The centurion who stood at the foot of the cross must have trembled as he realized the Divinity of the Son of God, and understood that he had been a partaker in His murder. It took an earthquake and blackened skies to open his eyes.

May God help us to shake the sinner, and let him see the blackness of sin, using the Law to also bring him to the foot of the cross and say with the centurion, "Truly, this was the Son of God!"

QUOTE FOR TODAY: "Jesus Christ burst from the grave and exploded in my heart." - Donna Hosford

* * *

MONDAY

READING: Hebrews 6:1-20

MEMORY VERSE: "For God is not unjust to forget your work and labor of love which you have shown toward His name, in that you have ministered to the saints, and do minister." Hebrews 6:10

It must have grieved the Apostle Paul to have to say, "I have fed you with milk, and not solid food; for until now you were not able to receive it, and even now you are still not able," to the Corinthian Church. Yet it seems to be a common thing that the Body of Christ has within it, those who never get out of the stroller. They prefer to be bottle fed than to feed themselves, that they might grow and walk themselves.

Paul had a similar message for the Hebrew Church --
"For though by this time you ought to be teachers, you need someone to teach you again the first principles of the oracles of God; and you have come to need milk and not solid food. For everyone who partakes only of milk is unskilled in the word of righteousness, for he is a babe." The Ephesians got a similar rebuke -- "That  we henceforth be no more children, tossed to and fro and carried about with every wind of doctrine, by the sleight of men, and cunning craftiness, whereby they lie in wait to deceive."

It brings great joy to the heart of a parent to see a child begin to feed himself. So, in the spiritual, it is a good thing when a Christian begins to feed himself on the Word of God.

When God sent manna from Heaven to the children of Israel, they had to collect it themselves. Moses didn't run around with a cart collecting it for them to spoon feed them. If that is the case, why do we need teachers in the local church?

Teachers are a gift from God to the Church to help us grow; all we need is the appetite to partake of the food. The shepherd leads the sheep to the green pasture, and the sheep do the eating.

When the Pastor takes the time to pray and study to find good pasture, the least we can do is to come prepared with a healthy appetite . . . God forbid that we should be satisfied with one or two meals a week. If we want to grow to the measure of the stature of the fullness of Christ, we need to daily eat the good manna from Heaven.

QUOTE FOR TODAY: "The more I study nature, the more I am amazed at the Creator." - Louis Pasteur

* * *

TUESDAY

READING: Exodus 16:1-22

MEMORY VERSE: "Whoever keeps his mouth and his tongue, keeps his soul from troubles." Proverbs 21:23

If we are not careful, it is very easy to be carried along with the negative murmurings of those who profess to be the people of God. In today's reading, Israel was taken along with the lusts of those who followed them out of Egypt. They longed for the appetite satisfiers of the land they had left.

God heard their murmurings and in His goodness, sent them bread from Heaven.

Can you imagine the excitement of gathering manna for the first time -- this was supernatural food! But it didn't take long for the novelty to wear off. Despite the fact that God had provided a miraculous manna meal, their murmurings were not muffled; they became bored.

We see from verse 16, that obedience was an important part of their partaking of this Heavenly food. They were told to gather a specific amount, and they were told when they could eat it. But they didn't listen to what Moses said, and some left it until morning; it bred worms and stunk.

Manna is a type of the Word. When we are first saved and eat the supernatural food from Heaven, there is an initial excitement. But it isn't long until we, like the children of Israel, become bored with the manna. If we don't couple obedience with what we read in the Word, the manna will go sour on us.

Sin will cause the Bible to stand as an accuser; and rather than being sweet, it will be bitter to us. Instead of sustaining us, it will condemn us; it will judge us on the Last Day. Only those who keep their hearts pure and thankful will appreciate the manna from Heaven. Only those who understand that a wilderness surrounds them, will be thankful for the faithful provision of God through His precious Word.

QUOTE FOR TODAY: "Life doesn't begin at forty, or at twenty, but at Calvary." - Elaine Kilgore

* * *

WEDNESDAY

READING: 1 John 5:1-21

MEMORY VERSE: "For whatever is born of God overcomes the world. And this is the victory that has overcome the world -- our faith." 1 John 5:4

In one of the most terrifying bird attacks on record, Italian glider pilot Antonio Beozzi fought a life and death battle with a golden eagle, 4,500 feet above the alps. The bird, for some reason, swooped straight at the glider and crashed through the cabin. Said Beozzi, "The eagle tore at me! I felt its claws in my flesh. I fought back, covered with blood." He was able to strangle the bird to death just as the craft dived out of control. He claimed later, " . . . it was the ultimate fear."

Adversity has a habit of striking us out of the blue. We can be peacefully gliding through life, when suddenly, the great eagle of adversity comes crashing through our cabin cover, bringing with it pain and fear.

Fortunately, God has given us weapons for such an attack. As satan tries to get his claws into our flesh, we have weaponry that will put a strangle-hold on him and render him helpless.

One of the devil's most vicious claws is fear. The Bible tells us that fear has "torment," and if you have ever been "gripped" by fear, you will know what it means. Yet the truth of the matter is, that fear should not be able to get through the cabin cover in the first place. That impregnable cover is the "shield of faith." As we believe and appropriate the many promises of God, our faith will quench all the fiery darts of the wicked. Think on this verse for a moment: "For the weapons of our warfare are not carnal, but mighty through God to the pulling down of strong holds" (2 Corinthians 10:4).

The next time we find ourselves peacefully gliding in God, let's make sure our shield cover is so thick that instead of smashing through, the enemy bounces off and thinks twice before he attacks again. But how do we get the density of faith that will cause the devil to flee from us? Simple -- "Submit yourself therefore to God, resist the devil, and he will flee from you."

QUOTE FOR TODAY: "How much more Christian love there would be if we didn't wait for death to release our reserves." - H.B. Andre

* * *

THURSDAY

READING: Romans 2:1-16

MEMORY VERSE: "For there is no respect of persons with God." Romans 2:11

A famous English General named Lou Wallace was once walking the streets of London when he and a friend were struck with the amount of church spires they could see. Wallace asked, "How long will so many people

continue to be deceived by the myth of Christianity?" His friend then encouraged him to write a book to disprove not only the claims of Christ, but also the very existence of the man Jesus.

After Wallace had gathered information from different sources, he made the mistake of turning to the Scriptures for more information. After two years of studying the New Testament, he fell to his knees and cried out to Jesus Christ, "My Lord and my God!" He then went on to write the epic novel "Ben Hur." By the way, if you have never seen the film "Ben Hur," you are missing the most wonderful portrayal of the life of Christ that you will ever see on the silver screen.

I wonder how many Lou Wallaces' are out there in the world? I wonder how many people have been duped by the facade of empty religious hypocrisy into thinking that Christianity is merely a myth for the masses? May God give us the wisdom and the compassion to reach out to them.

I heard the testimony of a young man recently, that challenged me as to how much I loved the lost. He shared with me how he was sitting at a dinner table while being witnessed to by a man and his wife. They both reasoned with him, but he still wouldn't turn his life over to the Savior. Then the man turned to him, and with tears in his eyes said, "If someone came in here with a gun and I was given the choice as to whether you or my wife should be shot, I would let my wife be killed and let you live; because she would go to Heaven, but you would go to Hell!" The young man glanced over at the wife to see her reaction. She nodded in total agreement. He then broke down and repented. Such an incident is a challenge isn't it?

QUOTE FOR TODAY: "The mass of men lead lives of quiet desperation." - Henry D. Thoreau

* * *

FRIDAY

READING: Romans 5:1-21

MEMORY VERSE: "God commended His love towards us, in that while we were yet sinners, Christ died for us." Romans 5:8

An Olympic gold medalist high-diving champion was once plagued with insomnia. As he tossed and turned upon his bed, he began thinking deeply about the success he had attained in his field (pool). He meditated on the many medals he had won.

To his dismay he realized that despite all his training and all the hard work, his success had not delivered what it

seemed to promise.

The excitement of winning, the photographers, and the medals still left him feeling empty inside. He was still the same person within.

Suddenly, he had had enough of lying there feeling sorry for himself. He decided to train once again. He arose from the bed and made his way to the diving pool. In the early hours of the morning, he walked through the corridors and, as he had his own key, he unlocked the door to the pool. He had made this trek so many times he didn't even bother to turn the pool lights on. In the semi-dark he climbed up the steps and walked out onto the diving board. He placed his feet together, stood perfectly upright, and pulled his arms back in a horizontal position.

As he stood there, he could see his shadow cast by the moonlight on the far wall. All he could see was a perfect cross. His mind immediately raced back to his Sunday School days. He remembered scriptures such as, "God commended his love toward us, in that, while we were yet sinners, Christ died for us." He remembered the Ten Commandments and suddenly felt unclean as he thought about how many he had transgressed. He knew that if he died in the state he was in, he would end up in Hell. Tears came to his eyes as he thought about the love displayed on that cross. He solemnly turned around, made his way back down the steps, dropped to his knees on the ground, and gave his life to Jesus Christ.

At daybreak he arose a new creature in Christ, knowing that his sins were forgiven. Once again he made his way back to the pool. To his utter astonishment, he found that it was completely empty. That previous evening the caretaker had emptied the pool, and was just beginning to refill it!

How different things would have been if he had seen the shadow of the cross, seen his sins, known of his fate and had said to himself --

"Tomorrow I'll give my life to God . . . !"

In the next 24 hours, approximately 200,000 people will pass through the door of death. Today may be the last opportunity we have to point them to the cross. May God give us a burden to open our mouths boldly and speak as we ought to.

QUOTE FOR TODAY: "Destiny waits in the hand of God, not in the hands of statesmen." - T.S. Elliot

* * *

SATURDAY

READING: Psalm 63:1-11

MEMORY VERSE: "Because you have been my help, therefore in the shadow of Your wings I will rejoice." Psalm 63:7

The Psalmist said, "Indeed, You have made my days as handbreadths, and my age is as nothing before You;

certainly every man at his best state is but vapor" (Psalm 39:5). Never before in the history of time, has man been so time conscious. The many watches and clocks remind us of time.

The dictionary says time is a "duration." According to the Bible, the time will come when time will no longer be in existence (Revelation 10:6). It is hard for us to think of an existence when no one will say, "What's the time?" or "How long will you be?" Everything will be in the present, if there is no future or past. Time is a dimension God created and put mankind into, and whether we like it or not, we are enslaved in its clutches, or should I say in the "hands of time."

It hurts our minds to try and understand that God dwells outside of time, but He dwells in *eternity*. If that sends the brain reeling, don't ask yourself what existed before God created eternity.

Look at these awesome scriptures: "For a thousand years in Your sight are like yesterday when it is past," and "Jesus Christ, is the same yesterday, today, and forever." He is timeless and therefore ageless. I am looking forward to that state into which God will place all those that love Him, to be clothed with a new body not subject to aging, pain, fear and all the other fruits of sin. It will be as the Bible says, an eternity (a long time) of "pleasure forevermore . . . world without end."

Meantime, the Scriptures do have a lot to say about time. They speak of God being a deliverer in time of trouble; they exhort us to exercise faith in times of fear; Hosea speaks of it being time to seek the Lord; Jesus spoke of "signs of the times;" Peter spoke of times of "refreshing;" and Paul spoke of a "time to awake out of sleep" for our salvation is nearer than when we first believed. In other words, it is time for the Church to redeem the time, to make or find the time to turn the world right side up for the Kingdom of God.

QUOTE FOR TODAY: "No man is free who cannot command himself." - Pythagorus

* * *

SUNDAY

READING: Psalm 23:1-6

MEMORY VERSE: "Yea, though I walk through the valley of the shadow of death, I will fear no evil; for You are with me, Your rod and Your staff comfort me." Psalm 23:4

Often we can read the most famous of the Psalms with an air of contempt. Most only read it at a funeral, so it carries connotations of death with it. It shouldn't because it's not about death. When it speaks of the "shadow of death," it's talking about the very opposite of what most think -- life. If I am in the shadow of a wall, I'm not *in* the wall, I'm just in close proximity to it. This life is the shadow of death. Death casts its black shadow over all of humanity; however, to them that "sat in the shadow of death, a light has sprung up." Those who come to the "Light of the world," see the power of light to banish darkness.

In this psalm, the promise to the believer is that God would "restore" the soul. What does that mean? The Hebrew is interesting; it means to "turn something back, but not necessarily to the starting point." Do you remember how the stranger, who was set upon by thieves and left half dead, had his life restored by the "good" Samaritan? So the sinner, whom satan has left half dead on the path of life, has his soul restored by Jesus Christ.

It also means "refreshing" and is tied in with the oil mentioned in verse 5. It is difficult for us who live in the Western world to appreciate the fact that in very warm countries, it was customary to anoint the body with oil to protect it from excessive perspiration. When mixed with perfume, the oil imparted a delightfully refreshing and invigorating sensation. Even today, athletes anoint their bodies as a matter of course before running a race. As the body therefore anointed with oil was refreshed, invigorated and better fitted for action, so is the effect of God's anointing upon the believer.

QUOTE FOR TODAY: "When one life is changed, the world is changed." - T.L. Johns

* * *

MONDAY

READING: Matthew 27:1-26

MEMORY VERSE: "What shall I do with this Jesus, who is called Christ?" Matthew 27:22

Will Judas go to Heaven? The issue becomes a little con-

fusing as one reads different versions of the Bible. For example the K.J.V. says, "Then Judas, which had betrayed Him, when he saw that He was condemned, repented himself, and brought again the thirty pieces of silver to the chief priests and elders saying, I have sinned in that I have betrayed innocent blood." Well, what does it mean by "repented himself?" The Good News versions says, "When Judas, the traitor, learnt that Jesus had been condemned, he repented and took back the thirty silver coins." So from these two versions, it looks as though Judas did repent. But let's look at the

Amplified Bible: "When Judas, His betrayer, saw that Jesus was condemned, he was afflicted in mind and troubled for his former folly; and with remorse, that is, an after care and little more than a selfish dread of the consequences, he brought back the thirty pieces of silver . . . " So then according to this version, Judas didn't repent.

This would seem to be verified by the warning Jesus gave of the actions of the betrayer-to-be, " . . . but woe unto that man by whom the Son of man is betrayed! It had been good for that man if he had not been born." Surely Jesus would not have used such harsh words about the fact that the betrayer would die by his own hands.

Well, in conclusion, we have to conclude that there is no conclusion until Judgment Day. Odds are, there will be many a Judas who found a place of repentance, and many a "saint" who never repented in the first place. In the mean time, each of us must examine our own hearts and make sure that we have obeyed the command to "make your calling and election sure."

QUOTE FOR TODAY: The person who said, "All good things must come to an end," can't have been a Christian.

* * *

TUESDAY

READING: 1 Samuel 30:1-20

MEMORY VERSE: "In all your ways acknowledge Him, and He shall direct your paths." Proverbs 3:6

The Bible is the most contemporary book in the world. It has answers to every human problem. The problem is, we often try to cover whatever is coming against us rather than triumphing in it. For example, in today's reading, David had every right to be in despair. He and his men arrived in their home town to find that every single thing they possessed had either been burned or stolen. Even their wives had been taken captive by  the enemy. If this wasn't bad enough, the men who were with David were so in despair they even spoke of stoning David. It was a nightmare.

It would have been quite understandable for David to say, "Dear God, what are you doing with my life? You promised I'd be a King, and now Saul seeks my life, I've lost my house and family and now my own men want to stone me!" But instead "David encouraged himself in the Lord his God." The Amplified Bible says he "strengthened" himself in God. What does that mean?

I think it means that David took his eyes off his dilemma and placed them on God. He reflected on how Samuel anointed him King, and how it thrilled his heart to think that God cared for him personally. He remembered the time he stood before Goliath and how God guided that stone and brought victory to Israel. David knew his God. He knew the deliverance God gives to those who trust in Him. He knew the faithfulness of His Creator. Perhaps he thought on how God delivered Israel from Egypt by opening the Red Sea, or on the principles he had learned from other portions of Scripture, all teaching that God is faithful, no matter how great the adversity.

It was in the faith-filled attitude that David heard the voice of the Lord, "Pursue . . . and recover all." Are you having a trial? Then learn from David, others in Scripture and multitudes down through history, that not only is God faithful to work out His purposes in your life, but He's very present right now to encourage you in your trial.

QUOTE FOR TODAY: Before Christ, a man loves things and uses people. After Christ, he loves people and uses things.

* * *

WEDNESDAY

READING: Genesis 24:1-28

MEMORY VERSE: "Commit your works to the Lord, and your thoughts will be established." Proverbs 16:3

Most of us are very familiar with the story of how Abraham sent out his servant to find a wife for his son Isaac; but do we see that beneath this story is a hidden picture of God, the Church and the Holy Spirit?

Abraham (God) says to the servant (The Holy Spirit) "But you shall go to my country and my family, and take a

wife for my son Isaac" (Isaac being a type of Christ). Remember how the Holy Spirit was first given? -- God sent Him to find a Bride for His Son. The Holy Spirit comes to us, seeking us out to be part of the Bride of Christ.

It was no coincidence that Abraham's servant, Eliezer (which means "God of help"), found Rebekah at a well. In Isaiah 12:3, salvation is actually spoken of as being a well.

Abraham said to his servant, "If this woman should not be willing to go along after you, then you will be clear from this oath." The Holy Spirit does not take unwilling souls . . . only "whosoever will."

Eliezer was a true servant. He was trustworthy (vs 2), he did not go without seeking God in prayer (vs 12), and he did not tend to his own needs until he had attended to his master's needs (vs 33). Isn't that the ministry of the Holy Spirit? -- totally faithful to the will and direction of the Father, never glorifying Himself, but glorifying the Son.

Throughout Scripture we see this truth echoed, that God is preparing a Bride for His Son. Those who have the "earnest of the Spirit" have been sealed as a "chaste virgin unto Christ." We are set aside from the world, pure and spotless through the blood of the Savior.

Don't let anything come between you and that day when we see Him as He is. Make it a habit (a good, humble, irreligious habit), to sincerely confess your sins daily. Speak to God about your lust problem, or your greed, or whatever, and ask His help in the future. Keep your garments spotless . . . *there is nothing so important.*

QUOTE FOR TODAY: "The great majority of men exist, but do not live." - Benjamin Disraeli

* * *

THURSDAY

READING: Philippians 4:1-19

MEMORY VERSE: "I can do all things through Christ who strengthens me." Philippians 4:13

Paul had a special love for the Philippian Church. It gave him fond memories of God's gracious Hand being extended in the salvation of Lydia, and the miracle of the great earthquake, which opened the doors of the Philippian jail and resulted in the salvation of the jailer and his family.

As Paul writes, he uses a strange term, "true yoke-fellow." Each of us should be able to claim the title true yokefellow, if we have obeyed the command of Jesus -- He said, "Take my yoke upon you." The problem with many who name the name of Christ is that they have never submitted to the yoke of Christ's Lordship, something which should be the natural outworking of repentance. They may act like yokefellows, but they are not "true" because they are the ones that are in control of their own lives.

The word "yoke" comes from a Greek word, "zugos,"

which means "a coupling of two things together." It denotes not only submission to Christ, but being submitted one to another.

In the passage, Paul encourages them to help each other and uses the term "fellow laborers." Oxen are yoked for the purpose of plowing, and that should be what we are doing when we become yoked with Jesus. We should be going where He goes, and doing what He does.

Then Paul ends the thought with the fact that the yokefellows' names are in the Book of Life, saying "rejoice in the Lord always." If we have repented and submitted ourselves to the yoke "that is easy," then we can have assurance that our names are written in the Book of Life, and that is the reason we rejoice always. Jesus said,

"Rejoice not because demons are subject to you, rejoice rather that your names are written in Heaven."

When Heaven is the object of your rejoicing, no one can take your joy from you.

QUOTE FOR TODAY: "Those who live in the Lord, never see each other for the last time." - German motto

* * *

FRIDAY

READING: Psalm 18:1-19

MEMORY VERSE: "The fool has said in his heart, There is no God." Psalm 14:1

A retired English film-studio manager, John Clogg, is one man in a thousand million with a very rare brain condition known as "double hemisphere action." As a result, he can simultaneously write different sentences with his right and left hands, and carry on a quite unconnected conversation at the same time. Leonardo da Vinci is believed to have had the same ability.

Clogg says of his talent, "It's never been a bit of use." However, the talent came in very handy for Leonardo. He wrote most of his writings "mirrored," so that those who actually saw his notes could not steal the ideas. His reason was that he was afraid that they would get into the wrong hands and be used for evil, rather than good.

He, like most of us, can see that the human race has as much capacity for evil as it has for good. The Bible calls it "sin," a word which has become very rare nowadays. That little word cuts close to the bone because it has the ability to involve all of us.

Look at all the evil that makes its way to the television news each evening -- the murders, rapes, corruption, theft, hatred, greed, etc, and yet this is just the tiny tip of a massive human iceberg.

I remember standing in a mall and seeing a crowd of people walk past me. Suddenly, someone pulled something from their pocket and also dropped a $2 bill on the ground. The person behind them swooped down, picked up the bill, turned 180 degrees and high-tailed into the distance. I couldn't believe what I'd seen! Can you imagine how evil this world would be if there was no restraint from civil law? Think about it.

If authorities said, "We believe that mankind is basically good, so there will be no punishment for any crime; in fact, no crime can ever be committed because there will be no law." That means, any man could rape any woman, anybody could rob any bank, and you and I could kill anyone we didn't like, etc, *without fear of retribution*. We are at a point of anarchy now, even with the threat of civil law hanging over the heads of would-be criminals. God only knows how wicked the human heart really is.

QUOTE FOR TODAY: "Failure is not sin. Faithlessness is." - Henrietta Mears

* * *

SATURDAY

READING: 1 Samuel 2:1-17

MEMORY VERSE: "Train up a child in the way he

should go, and when he is old, he will not depart from it."
Proverbs 22:6

Most of us are familiar with the story of Hannah. She
was at first unable to bear children, but God answered her
earnest prayer and gave her Samuel. Hannah wisely dedicated her child to the Lord even before she conceived. She

kept her promise by
giving Samuel to Eli the
priest for a ministry
within the House of the
Lord. This happened
when Samuel was a
child.

As we continue to
read further into the
Book of Samuel, we see
that Eli had two sons,
Hophni and Phinehas.
Both of these young
mean are called "sons of
Belial," which says something about their character. They
were full of rebellion, greed, sexual perversion, and
obviously, as the Scriptures tell us, "They knew not the
Lord." In fact, we are told that their sin was very great in
the sight of the Lord.

God held Eli responsible for the moral position of his
sons. The Bible says he honored them above the Lord, and
that his sons "made themselves vile, and he restrained them
not."

It seems that Eli didn't really care about the eternal
welfare of his boys. If he had, he would have laid the rod

on their "hindermost part." He didn't bother to drive the foolishness from them with the "rod of correction," and they retained it into adulthood.

It would seem that Hannah and her husband trained Samuel in the way he should go, even before they gave him to Eli. Samuel was not corrupted by Eli's sons of the devil. There is a very valuable lesson for parents and parents to be. All the hard work is done in the early days, from 1-7 years.

I always try and encourage parents who discipline their children when they show signs of rebellion. We practically wore out the pants of our first child. He became a good example for our other two kids, in fact we hardly had to chasten them. We put a total of 3,000 family devotional readings into Jacob, and after 18 years, it suddenly paid off. He did all the right things, went to church, read his Bible daily, never cussed, was always respectful, but in February of 1990, he dropped to his knees in his bedroom and repented. What a change!

So, let's take a valuable lesson from Eli's mistake and not make the same one.

QUOTE FOR TODAY: "It is easier to denature plutonium than to denature the evil spirit of man." - Albert Einstein

* * *

SUNDAY

READING: Galatians 4:1-18

MEMORY VERSE: "God has sent forth the Spirit of His

Son into your hearts, crying out, Abba, Father!" Galatians 4:6

If you take the time to have a close look at the vastness of this universe with its unnumbered galaxies, you will see what a tiny speck this massive earth is in comparison. Then what tiny dots each of us are in comparison to this earth. How great Almighty God must be, not only to have created it all, but to be concerned with each of us as individuals. I often feel utterly over-whelmed when I think what God must be like, to a point of tears and even a fearful awe. Yet we are allowed to call Him "Father." No Eastern religion even dares to do that. Plato and other philosophers spoke of the Creator being, the "Father of the universe," but never a father who loves and cares for his children. Such a thought was and is unthinkable to the Christian. Most of us know when the Bible says we are to call God, "Abba, Father," that the word Abba means "Daddy," and breaks down the thought that God is an austere, unapproachable father figure. No, He is portrayed to us in Scripture as being kind and loving, whose "good pleasure" it is to "give us the Kingdom."

In the garden of Gethsemane Jesus began His prayer with the words, "Abba, Father." In His distress and agony,

He knew He could draw near to His dear, loving Father. Cultivate your relationship with God to a point where you can, in a sense, climb up on His knee and speak to Him about what is worrying you, or even just to sit on His lap and love and admire Him. John Bunyan said, "Although it be an easy thing to say "Our Father" with the mouth, there are very few that can, in the spirit, say the first two words of that prayer; that is, call God their Father, knowing what it is to be born again, and having experienced that they are begotten of the Word of God."

QUOTE FOR TODAY: "When a Christian is winning souls, he isn't messing around with sin." - George L. Smith

* * *

MONDAY

READING: Romans 12:1-21

MEMORY VERSE: "Do not be conformed to this world, but be transformed by the renewing of your mind, that you may prove what is that good and acceptable and perfect will of God." Romans 12:2

Did you know that the term "brain-washing" is a reasonably recent one? It was first used by an American journalist named Edward Hunter during the Korean war as a translation of a Chinese colloquialism, "hsi nao," which means "to wash the brain."

Although the term "brain-washed" is often leveled at Christians in a derogatory sense, the words "brain washed" are apt to the true meaning of what happens to the believer at regeneration. Those of us who have drunk in the impurities of the world before conversion, have had our mind become like a blocked drain; and now we need to obey the Scriptures which tell us to clear the drain out -- ". . . be not conformed

to this world, but be transformed by the renewing of the mind, that you may prove what is that good and acceptable and perfect will of God." The Word washes our minds as it passes through. It cleanses and purifies the filth it once embraced. This is the analogy the Bible uses when it speaks of the Church being purified, " . . . that He might sanctify and cleanse her with the washing of the water by the Word, that He might present her to Himself a glorious church, not having spot or wrinkle or any such thing, but that she should be holy and without blemish."

To give our mind to the washing of the Word, is to relieve it of the guilt, the weight, and the stain of sin. As we read the Word, we see how our lives don't match the love we ought to have, or the devotion to prayer we should have, so we confess our sins; and the effect will be a natural growth in our walk.

As Christians, it should be a number one priority to make sure we are clean in the sight of God. Paul spoke of having a conscience "void of offense toward God and man."

However, if we only rely on our conscience, without the light of God's Word, we may be walking in sin without knowing it. For example, as a new Christian, I saw nothing wrong with taking a shortcut through the parking lot of an alcohol retailer. It saved me time; but the Bible told me to avoid the "appearance of evil," as it may have looked to some that I was stopping by for a drink. The conscience only brought conviction in the light of the Word.

One of the safest ways to make sure you keep free from sin, is to read your Bible daily, and let the Word cleanse your mind, and then your Christian life will be a walk of holiness to the Lord.

QUOTE FOR TODAY: It's not what you eat that counts, but what eats you (see Hebrews 12:15).

* * *

TUESDAY

READING: 2 Corinthians 4:1-18

MEMORY VERSE: "For we preach not ourselves, but Christ Jesus the Lord, and ourselves your servants for Jesus' sake." 2 Corinthians 4:5

"Think not that I am come to send peace on the earth; I am not come to send peace but a sword. For I am come to set a man at variance against his father and the daughter against her mother, and the daughter-in-law against her mother-in-law." Matthew 10:34-35.

When Jesus spoke these words He was actually quoting

from Micah 7:6, which was a passage referring to the time when the Kingdom of God would invade this dark world, when the light would spring up in the midst of those who hate the light. If you know God, you will more than likely know the cold reality of being divided by the Sword of the Lord from those whom you love. It is a division real to both parties, a division of those in light and those in darkness.

In fact, salvation is continually compared to light in the darkness. Just as the Sword of the Spirit (God's Word) divided the light from the darkness in the beginning, so that same Word divided in the incarnation. Wherever Jesus went, He shined as a light and divided the darkness. His words were quick and powerful, life itself. His words bring mercy or judgment to the hearers, dividing as sheep or goats. We either gather or scatter. This happened in John Chapter 7, when Jesus spoke the Word -- "So there was a division among the people because of Him." In Chapter 9 "Others said, How can a man that is a sinner do such miracles? And there was a division among them." Then in Chapter 10, "There was a division therefore again among the Jews for these sayings." Light doesn't mix with darkness. As we draw closer to the coming of the Lord, things are going to get darker and there will be a clearer division among those who obey God and those who merely give

Him lip service. Let's trim our lamps and let our lights shine. Light is more powerful than darkness, and wherever you take the light, there will be division; but the more who come to Christ, the less darkness there will be -- "But all things that are exposed are made manifest by the light, for whatever makes manifest is light. Therefore He says, Awake, you who sleep, arise from the dead, and Christ shall give you light" (Ephesians 5:13-14).

QUOTE FOR TODAY: The Lord sometimes takes us into troubled waters, not to drown us, but to cleanse us.

* * *

WEDNESDAY

READING: Colossians 3:1-25

MEMORY VERSE: "Whatever you do, do it heartily, as to the Lord, and not to men." Colossians 3:23

A 51 year old housewife, Mrs. Marva Drew of Waterloo, Iowa, typed out every number from one to a million after her son's teacher told him it was impossible to count up to one million. It took her five years and a total of 2,473 sheets of typing paper.

There are, perhaps, three ways of looking at such an act -- steadfastness, stubbornness or stupidity. It does, however, show the lengths some people will go to, to prove a point. She wanted to back up her beliefs with action.

This brings to mind the objection of many a non-Christian to the Christian. They say, "But what if the Bible is wrong when it speaks of an after-life?" Simple. If there is no after-life, we won't even know that we were wrong, will we? Then even the most ardent skeptic won't have the pleasure of saying, "I told you so!" But if the Bible is right, and after death, "The Judgment," then he will lose his most prized possession, his very soul!

Well, do we have to wait around until we die before we find out the truth? No, we don't have to remain in the darkness of our ignorance. We need not have the weak philosophy of Blood, Sweat and Tears who sang, "We say there is no Heaven, and we pray there is no Hell . . . but if it's peace you find in dying, then only my dying will tell."

The Bible teaches that there is not only life after death, but there is life before death. It is in the life we receive before death, that is the proof of the life after death. When someone "comes to Christ," they don't receive a religion but the very source of life itself . . . the life of Jesus Christ. The Apostle Paul put it this way, "When Christ Who is our life shall appear, then shall you also appear with Him in glory."

God seals each believer with the Holy Spirit as a token of His good faith, that He will keep His Word to us. If you had an uncle who said he was going to give you a million dollars, and as a token of his good faith he was giving you $100,000 right now, wouldn't that be adequate proof that he meant what he said? -- Then how much more should we believe God?

QUOTE FOR TODAY: "Unless a man undertakes more than he possibly can do, he will never do all he can do." - Henry Drummond

* * *

THURSDAY

READING: Galatians 5:1-26

MEMORY VERSE: "If we live in the Spirit, let us also walk in the Spirit." Galatians 5:25

I was in the process of publishing a new book called, Murphy's Law of Flying, so I watched other travellers board the flight with interest as we awaited takeoff on route to L.A. I have flown over 400 times and found that not only do I have tired arms, but air travel is the ideal place for Murphy's Law (what can go wrong, will go wrong) to abound.

One consolation about this flight was the complimentary breakfast, which I was looking forward to. It turned out to be omelette, stuffed with onion, peppers and chives -- why did they leave out the garlic? Obviously this was an attempt to destroy my marriage (Sue won't come near me when I eat onions; they may build me up physically, but they sure let me down socially).

I don't think I have ever heard such a helpful captain as the one on this flight. He was continually pointing out wonderful sights for the passengers to see, on the left side of the plane. I was seated on the right side. What's more, I had one of those one in a hundred seats which didn't have a window.

Immediately after takeoff, the gentleman in front of me pushed his seat back, leaving about an inch of his window for me to see through. I could clearly see part of the wing. Again the captain started raving about the view . . . on the left-hand side. He was so excited about it, he even banked the plane so the passengers could see the sight more clearly. Meanwhile, the right side got a nice view of the sky.

Ah, a break! The man in front put his seat in the upright position. I leaned forward and took in the view. It was amazing to look down on God's handiwork. I leaned my head up close to the window. I could see the . . . suddenly back came the seat, almost trapping my head between the seat and the window ledge.

This seemed to amuse the passenger next to me. The wife of the guy in front wanted to see the view and had leaned over, so back went his seat. Never mind. I would talk to the happy chappy next to me.

I'd prayed that God would give me opportunity to share my faith with him, so I asked what he did for a job. As I did so, I casually bit into a piece of cold breakfast muffin. He said "Sunglasses representative . . . what do you do?" With muffin sticking to the roof of my mouth I said, "I'm an author."

Unfortunately, he didn't speak muffin and thought I said, "I'm an orphan." Oh dear. I did get to witness to the guy; however, I missed seeing the Grand Canyon. That was on the left side of the plane. I claimed Romans 8:28, "All things work together for good, to those who love God and are called according to his purposes," and was thankful for air travel; because it sure beats walking.

QUOTE FOR TODAY: "No man is so virtuous as to marry a wife only to have children." - Martin Luther

* * *

FRIDAY

READING: Luke 10:1-37

MEMORY VERSE: "Not withstanding in this rejoice not, that the spirits are subject to you; but rather rejoice because your names are written in Heaven." Luke 10:20

If there is one thing that can ruin today, it's regrets about yesterday. Sadly, tragedies of yesterday are gone forever, and no amount of regret can change that fact.

I vividly remember an incident in my late teens. Although the pain is gone, the memory lingers. I had decided to go for a quick surf just before our evening meal late one Saturday afternoon. As soon as I picked up my surfboard my dog started "doing his thing;" he would bark and run around in frantic circles of excitement as the thought of the beach came to his canine mind. As we walked together, the thought of all those seagulls scattering at his every bark was just too much for him . . . he had to run ahead of me.

It was a hot Saturday and the roads were busy, so I called him back once, twice, then again, louder, then louder, but it was no good -- he rushed onto the road and was hit by a station wagon. It was as though I saw it happen in slow motion, his body spun out under the back of the car. All I can remember is dropping my expensive new surfboard onto the sidewalk and running onto the road without looking to the left or right, picking up the dog and rushing home.

As I sat at our gate, nursing a semi-conscious bleeding animal, the driver approached me. He muttered something about it not being his fault, then he burst into tears as he leaned on my shoulder. We rushed the dog to the veterinarian clinic, but much to my sorrow he had to be "put down," as they say.

Over the following weeks I relived that horrible incident within my mind over and over again, "If only I hadn't gone surfing . . . if only the dog had obeyed me; if only . . . if only."

Even though it was just a dog, he was special to me.

What about the wife who encourages her husband to take a break and go on a fishing trip on which he drowns, or the mother who sends her child across a road and sees him killed, or the pills that aren't locked away or the swimming pool gate left open? What about the giant "*If only*" which plagues the guilty party? To them there is only one answer . . . the love and grace of Almighty God; He alone can heal such pain and give the grace to forgive ourselves.

Saul of Tarsus was one man who could have been plagued by regret. He had been a zealous persecutor of the Christian church, actually having Christians killed because of their faith in Jesus. Yet, by the grace (i.e. the supernatural ability of God), Paul could say, (and so can we), "Forgetting that which is behind, I press toward the mark of the prize of the high calling of God in Christ Jesus."

QUOTE FOR TODAY: "Revival is nothing else than a new beginning of obedience to God." - Charles G. Finney

* * *

SATURDAY

READING: Mark 16:1-20

MEMORY VERSE: "And He said to them, Go into all the world and preach the Gospel to every creature." Mark 16:15

At the end of Chapter 5 of the Book of Hebrews, Paul (presumed to be the author) has some stern words for those who lack maturity as Christians. He said that they were dull

of hearing, or to put it in modern language, they were "dense." He went on to say that they should have been sharpening their teeth on meat, rather than drinking mere milk. The King James Version puts it this way -- "But strong meat belongs to them that are of full age, even those who, by reason of use, have their senses exercised to discern both good and evil." In other words, Christian maturity is discerned by the believer's ability to distinguish between good and evil. For instance, the shallow nature of my first few weeks as a Christian was evidenced by the fact that I didn't have any opinion about nudist camps. I had heard justification for their immoral behavior, that they were "health camps" and "natural living," or that they were following in Adam and Eve's bare foot prints.

Well, were Adam and Eve the first nudists? Obviously they were, but let me qualify the statement. I heard an interesting thought recently about our first Mom and Dad.

Isn't it true that when you see a plucked duck or turkey, something seems to be missing? The bird just doesn't look right without its feathers. In the same way, the thought of Adam and Eve running around naked in the Garden of Eden just doesn't seem right.

However, we must remember that our imaginations are limited by the fall.

Do you also remember when Moses came down from talking to God, how his skin shone with such a radiancy that the children of Israel couldn't even look at him? The same thing happened to Jesus' face after He was transfigured. Is it not probable that, because Adam and Eve were in continual communion with the God of Glory, their skin also shone like that of Moses and Jesus? Can you imagine the other creatures in the garden saying, "Look out . . . guard your eyes, here comes the supreme creation of God, Adam and Eve!" I'm not saying we should form a new doctrine, or start the "First National Church of the Shining Skinites," what I'm saying is, that this is an interesting alternative to the "plucked chicken" thought, and would do away with the paintings we continually see of Adam and Eve standing behind bushes or with leaves falling at just the right places.

Whatever the case may be, those who are trusting in the mercy of our God, will someday be transformed from this old, fallen, corruptible body, into a brand new, incorruptible, glorious body, which will no doubt shine for eternity.

QUOTE FOR TODAY: "When you cannot remove an object, plow around it. But keep plowing." - Megiddo Message

* * *

SUNDAY

READING: John 15:1-27

MEMORY VERSE: "If you abide in Me and My words

abide in you, you will ask what you desire, and it shall be done for you." John 15:7

"Punk" hairstyles lasted longer than I thought they would. I must admit that I was as shocked as the next person, when I saw my first weird hairstyle. It was actually in the bathroom mirror which my Mom had taken off the wall to show me the effect of soapy hair pulled skyward. That was when I was about five years old, but that's the precise method used by most young people who want to stand out in a crowd. Others dye their hair green, shave it off, shave half of it off or shave two thirds off, leaving a mohawk hedge down the middle.

Why do young people do such things? There are a number of reasons: some want to rebel against society, others are bored, or insecure. They lack identity and this is their way of belonging to something. They are no longer lost in a huge flock of ducks; they are different -- people notice them, even if they are ugly ducklings.

When I look back on my teenage years, I also lacked a sense of identity; I, too, was insecure. I was part of that great Hippie movement which rebelled against society. I was shaped by the huge hands of Hippie non-conformity to conform to a lifestyle that we all thought was different. I wore leather sandals, Levis jeans, grew my hair long and liked particular types of music . . . just like the millions of other non-conformists. Despite that, we all did feel different and we all did have a sense of identity, doing something we felt had never been done before.

No doubt today's teenagers feel exactly the same -- so will tomorrows. But everything offered by the world is merely a mirage. It seems to promise, but it never delivers. The Hippies of my day, who so believed in a free lifestyle, are either disillusioned suburbanites, rich "Yuppies" who by their lifestyle have proved to be "Hippiecrites," dead drug addicts, or they have become Christians. How thankful I am that I, along with many others, became a Christian. In doing so, I found what I was looking for. I found that security in Jesus and that identity I so lacked, when I came to the Savior.

QUOTE FOR TODAY: "Sin is not hurtful because it is forbidden; but sin is forbidden because it is hurtful." - Benjamin Franklin

* * *

MONDAY

READING: Acts 1:1-26

MEMORY VERSE: "But you shall receive power when the Holy Spirit comes upon you; and you shall be witnesses to Me in Jerusalem, and in all Judaea and Samaria, and to the end of the earth." Acts 1:8

Before becoming a Christian, temptation was something I seldom wrestled with. If sin came my way, like most non-Christians, I would just yield to its power. Selfishness, lust and greed had free entry into my life. But on becoming a Christian, I began to endure a "great fight of afflictions." Instead of yielding to lust, I began to fight it and found that I was, as the Bible says, in the midst of a mighty battle.

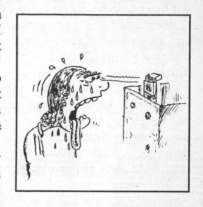

The battle is similar to a man who smokes forty cigarettes a day. Smoking is no problem to him; if he wants one, he just has one . . . no big deal. But when he tries to give the habit up, he finds he doesn't have a habit, the habit has him. His hands begin to shake, his body begins to perspire, and he begins to withdraw from the drug. All of a sudden, the battle begins. The cigarettes, which were no problem when given free course, now begin to show how much grip they had on the person.

Sin's grip begins to tighten as the Christian resists its power. The battle begins between what the Bible calls the flesh and the spirit; but praise God, He has given us His Holy Spirit so that we don't fight the battle alone.

I once heard something that has really encouraged me when it comes to resisting temptation, and that is the thought that our Heavenly Father smiles every time He sees one of His children resist the temptation to sin. Many

Christians come under condemnation because they think that temptation is sin, but the Scriptures tell us that Jesus was "tempted on all points as you and I, yet without sin." Satan tempted Jesus in a number of areas, yet Jesus resisted him and remained free from sin. If we do yield to temptation and fall into sin, we must not remain in such a state, but immediately cry out to God for cleansing and forgiveness, because sin will deceive and harden the heart against God. Hand in hand with the "deceitfulness of sin" comes what the Bible calls "an evil heart of unbelief." Most who backslide deceive themselves with the ostrich theory of, "I don't believe in God, Heaven, Hell or Judgment Day."

Let's not for one minute allow sin to have reign in our mortal bodies, but resist temptation, because he who has the hope of everlasting life "purifies himself."

QUOTE FOR TODAY: "It is in recognizing the actual presence of God that we find prayer no longer a chore, but a supreme delight." - Gordon Lindsay

* * *

TUESDAY

READING: Romans 10:1-21

MEMORY VERSE: "That if you confess with your mouth the Lord Jesus and believe in your heart that God has raised Him from the dead, you will be saved." Romans 10:9

Did you know, that when a rabbit cornered by a snake sits motionless, it is not "hypnotized" by the attacker; it simply knows by instinct that the snake's weak eyes cannot distinguish a still animal from a lifeless one. The rabbit's safety lies in its stillness.

Moses related such a truth to the children of Israel when they found themselves cornered by their enemies with no way out. He said, "Stand still and see the salvation of God." There is a great truth in the thought, "when there is no way out, try looking up." He who stands still and looks solely to the Lord for deliverance will find that indeed, "God is our refuge and strength; a very present help in trouble."

Satan has many wiles, in fact, that word "wiles" in Ephesians Chapter 6 comes from a Greek word "METHO-DEIAS," the word from which we derive the English word, "method." Some of the enemy's methods include attempting to bring doubt to the Christian by causing him to question the promises of God. In *Pilgrim's Progress,* Pilgrim found himself in Doubting Castle, harassed by the merciless "GIANT DESPAIR." The only way out of that cold castle, filled with dead men's bones, was to take hold of the "Key of Promise" and use it. Other wiles of the devil include division in the body of Christ, temptation, error, and one subtle tactic, of which I have to stay clear, "acting on impulse." Fools indeed, rush in where angels fear to tread. Satan caused Eve to act quickly without any thought of the implications of her actions. Things would be different if she had been still and waited for the counsel of God.

Many people are no longer alive because they didn't weigh up the implication of their actions, they acted upon impulse summed up in the bumper sticker which reads, "UNDERTAKERS, KEPT BUSY BY OVERTAKERS."

QUOTE FOR TODAY: "To believe in Heaven is not to run away from life; it is to run toward it." - Joseph D. Blinco

* * *

WEDNESDAY

READING: 2 Corinthians 5:1-21

MEMORY VERSE: "Knowing therefore the terror of the Lord, we persuade men." 2 Corinthians 5:11

The Bible tells us that when Paul arrived at Athens he came across a very strange thing. It says, "for all the Athenians and strangers who were there spent their time in nothing else, but either to tell or hear some new thing." It is almost unbelievable that grown men would sit around like a group of ladies in a knitting circle gossiping about what's new. Who would believe that anybody could be so consumed with such a pastime, yet, let's take a quick look at modern man.

In this day and age, it's the normal practice to produce large multi-page publications, printed every morning or evening, seven days a week, entirely devoted to telling of new things; they are called *news-papers*.

Over an hour each night, on prime time television,

programs concentrate solely on reporting new things, in fact that program is called the News. Radio also acknowledges man's craving to hear of new things with its news broadcasts and news flashes. Now before we proceed further, I must admit that I enjoy watching, reading and listening to the news, but

some years ago, I noticed that almost every new thing that was being told was a negative thing -- murder, violence, war, suicide, crime, accidents, etc. My own outlook, even as a Christian, was becoming negative and pessimistic. I also noticed that you could trace many a marriage breakup to a communication breakdown. Almost always, somewhere in there amongst the confusion, was newspaper or television abuse.

Personally I've found that the world still carries on with its activities and problems without me burying my head in negativity.

Yet multitudes feel that they must catch the numerous radio bulletins and read every one of the 350,000 words in the average newspaper, sadly, at the expense of a marriage or family life.

I'm impressed with the unique way a friend of mine got the message across to her husband. She made a hole in the middle of the newspaper put it over her head and made her entrance with the words -- "I thought that if I was wearing the evening newspaper you may notice me."

QUOTE FOR TODAY: "Revival is the rush of the Spirit into a body that threatens to become a corpse." - D. M. Panton

* * *

THURSDAY

READING: Ephesians 3:1-21

MEMORY VERSE: "That Christ may dwell in your hearts through faith; that you, being rooted and grounded in love . . ." Ephesians 3:17

Studies have shown that young children prefer to listen to adults who speak quickly. The average child prefers to listen to words spoken at about one hundred seventy-five per minute or even two hundred, if you're not rushed. They do not like being spoken to slowly. These conclusions came out of a study in which children used a machine which allowed them to regulate the speed of recorded speech without distortion. Blind children were an exception; they preferred even faster talk

at around two hundred seventy-five words per minute, perhaps because they suffered no visual distractions.

There would seem to be a rather obvious lesson here for Christians. The mind can take in much more when not distracted by other things.

In the parable of the sower, Jesus spoke of the seed which was choked by thorns as being: "such as hear the word, and the cares of this world, and the deceitfulness of riches, and the lusts of other things entering in, choke the Word, and it becomes unfruitful." Let's not be deceived into thinking that this is confined to the unsaved who come under the sound of the Gospel and yet have the seed of life choked by thorns.

This experience can be ours as we sit under the sound of the Word within our own church or even as we sit with our loved ones during family devotions. The cares of this world can slowly creep into our minds and choke that precious seed of God's Word.

When the world would encourage us to "take care," we need to understand that God tells us to be "careful for nothing." Instead of taking care, we need to "cast our care" because the Bible says, "Cast all your care on Him for He cares for you."

Care is just another name for anxiety, concern or worry. Before you come under the sound of the Word of God "cast your cares upon the shoulders of our Mighty God; the care of that financial problem, of that sick child, or that weakness that so easily besets us, and then rest in the love of God, leaving Him in His infinite wisdom to deal with the problem and leave the soil of your heart free to receive the seed of life.

QUOTE FOR TODAY: "The Bible redirects my will, cleanses my emotions, enlightens my mind and quickens my total being." - E. Stanley Jones

* * *

FRIDAY

READING: Philippians 1:1-30

MEMORY VERSE: "For to me to live is Christ, and to die is gain." Philippians 1:21

In the book of Hebrews, the writer says, "We ought to give more earnest heed to the things which we have heard, least at any time we should let them slip." The Amplified Bible gives us an even closer look at what the Scripture is saying: "We ought to pay much closer attention than ever to the truths that we have heard, least in any way we drift past them and slip away." In other words, if we do lose grip . . . we're the ones that fall.

The Scriptures are full of admonitions to hearken, to hearken diligently, and to give earnest heed, probably because most of the time our minds are a little like a strainer; things just seem to slip through them. I remember reading somewhere, or then again I may have heard someone say, that we forget up to 90% of what we hear . . . or was it 80% . . . I can't really remember the exact percentage, which does prove the point.

If we do want to grow in Christ to maturity, we must recognize this weakness and, as it were, begin to patch up the holes in the strainer. How often do imaginations and other thoughts crowd into our minds as we sit under a preacher to hear the Word of God expounded? I remember in school feeling quite proud of how I could fool the teacher by looking as though I was listening, when I was in fact miles away.

I even learned to nod in agreement, when I didn't have the faintest idea what he was saying. The trouble was, I was the one who was being cheated and the same applies with the Word of God . . . if we don't eat, we starve.

When Paul wrote to Timothy he said, "If you put the brethren in remembrance of these things," while Peter used phrases such as, "I stir up your pure minds by way of remembrance," because both knew the strainer tendency of the human mind.

We need to be reminded constantly who we are in Christ, what we have in Him, who we are fighting and what to fight with.

The whole question really comes back to the fact that he who hearkens to God, hearkens for his own good . . . I mean, would you let your mind wander off into other things while the Will of a rich relative was being read? Would you stay in a dream if you heard your name mentioned? I know you wouldn't.

QUOTE FOR TODAY: "A saint is never consciously a

saint; a saint is consciously dependant on God." - Oswald Chambers.

* * *

SATURDAY

READING: Galatians 2:1-21

MEMORY VERSE: "I am crucified with Christ; neverthe-less I live; yet not I but Christ lives in me; and the life which I now live in the flesh I live by the faith of the Son of God, who loved me, and gave himself for me." Galatians 2:20

It seems that it isn't too hard to convince a non-Christian of the existence of sin. One just has to open the daily newspaper and point out all the hatred, crime and corrup-tion in the world, then say that the Bible calls such wrong-doing, sin. But to bring the reality of sin to a personal level and try to get that person to acknowledge their own individ-ual sinfulness, well, that's a different story. It's always the "other person" who is responsible for the problems of the world.

Right from the beginning, man has sought to "pass the buck" when it comes to sin. When God confronted Adam about personal guilt, it would seem that Adam pointed to Eve as the guilty party. Genesis Chapter 3 tells us that Adam said, "The woman who *You* gave to be with me, she gave me of the tree, and I did eat." Yet, there is another way in which one can read Adam's words and see to whom he was passing the buck. "And the man said, The woman who You gave to be with me, she gave me of the tree, and I did eat." Adam was also seeking to blame God for the mess he had gotten himself into.

Of course the nature of the Adamic race hasn't changed one bit. Man still seeks to blame God for his own mess. No doubt you have heard ones site God as the cause of starvation in Africa. "If God is a God of love, why does He let people starve to death?" Yet, they are not very interested in the fact that  to feed, house, clothe and educate the entire world for a period of twelve months would cost the phenomenal amount of 17 billion dollars . . . approximately the same amount the world spends on armorments every two weeks!

The truth of the matter is, that if man would repent and come to know the God of love, he wouldn't let his neighbor starve to death while he himself grows fat as he stuffs himself with the providence of God. Foolish man, in blind arrogance, imagines that he sees a speck in the eye of God, while to say a log is in his own eye is a gross understatement.

The book of Proverbs tells us that God longs to give humanity the knowledge needed for this world to live in peace and harmony.

God, in His love, calls to rebellious humanity:

"Turn you at my reproof; behold, I will pour out my Spirit unto you, I will make known my words unto you." The comparative few who hearken to those words come to know the joy of sins forgiven; but sadly most of humanity, like a senseless animal, insists upon biting the Hand of God that so graciously feeds it.

QUOTE FOR TODAY: "If I could hear Christ praying for me in the next room, I would not fear a million enemies. Yet distance makes no difference, He is praying for me." - Robert Murray McCheyne

* * *

SUNDAY

READING: Colossians 4:1-18

MEMORY VERSE: "Continue earnestly in prayer, being vigilant in it with thanksgiving." Colossians 4:2

I wonder if you are aware of the fact that many Biblical names bring out the character of that personality. Such is the case for the New Testament word "devil." The word devil means accuser or slanderer, and that aptly describes two of the many "wiles of the devil." Many Christians are held back from being effective for the Kingdom of God, purely because they chose to believe the lies of the devil rather than the truths of the Word of God.

When the prodigal son returned from feeding pigs, his father covered his filth with a "robe;" speaking to us of the robe of righteousness which God gives to every believer.

The problem is that many of us keep looking under the robe to see what God no longer sees. For instance, what is your immediate reaction to the question, "What does God think of you?" Many of us are tempted to hang our head in shame and say, "I'm sure God frowns upon me, I'm so full of

greed, lust, and pride." Yet, God has made those of us who walk according to His Word, "every whit clean." He has given us the purity of the robe of righteousness. To continually look under the robe, is to cheat ourselves, and undermine the redemptive work of the Son of God. Jesus poured out His life's blood on that cruel cross so that you and I might be spotless in the sight of God. If we do fall, through the weakness of human flesh, cleansing is only a confession away. God knows our every weakness and has made total provision for it.

The problem arises when we are continually plagued by one sin or even a number of besetting sins. Time does not allow me to elaborate on the continual wickedness of my own flesh but I do know that the accuser is always there to bring me into condemnation -- "Who do you think you are, with all your sins, that you can stand in the presence of God!" But the Bible says, "Submit to God, resist the devil and he will flee from you." To submit means to surrender yourself to God -- and that includes believing His Word.

When I get continual godless thoughts flooding my mind, I talk to the Lord about the problem. He knows what's going on anyway.

Some years ago, I was riding along on my Honda 50 motorcycle, when an angry German shepherd dog rushed out of a driveway and began to chase me.

As he barked, growled and snapped at the back wheel, I had the revelation "greater is he that I am riding, than he that is chasing."

Then, much to the amazement of the dog, I stopped the bike, turned it around, and chased the surprised animal up the road.

Christian, don't put up with the lies and accusations of the devil for another minute. He is your enemy. He came to kill, steal and destroy. He is the author of rebellion against God. Turn on him with holy vengeance and resist him "steadfast in the faith," then stand tall in the righteousness of Christ and offer yourself as a soldier outfitted for battle in the service of the King.

QUOTE FOR TODAY: "The only thing necessary for evil to triumph is for good men to do nothing." - Edmund Burke

* * *

MONDAY

READING: 1 Thessalonians 5:1-28

MEMORY VERSE: "And the very God of peace sanctify you wholly; and I pray God your whole spirit and soul be preserved blameless unto the coming of our Lord Jesus

Christ." 1 Thessalonians 5:23

Some time ago, our family had a number of chickens. Now there were obvious advantages of having our own feathered friends; one being, that food scraps turned into fresh eggs. Such blessings however, were hardly worth the experience of being awakened in the early hours of a summer morning by loud, offensive fowl language.

We were often fascinated by the goings on in the chicken house. Chickens have what is known as a "pecking order," that is, they sort out who is boss. On studying our bunch we noticed that three of them had a lack of feathers around the tail area; in fact, one of them was beginning to look like one of the supermarket variety -- she was so lacking in covering.

The fourth one had every feather neatly in place. Whenever she wanted food or drink and one of the other three was in the way, a quick peck on the unprotected rear would clear the way.

Such is typical of this world with its oppressive system. Those who are clothed with the protective feathers of finance, find themselves at the top of the pecking order, yet God in His infinite wisdom and grace has totally reversed this cruel system. In this world, money speaks. It can buy almost anything, anything but peace of mind and peace with God. The Bible tells us that "riches profit not in the Day of Wrath, but righteousness delivers from death." Simon the magician was rebuked for his wickedness in thinking that the gift of God could be purchased. God doesn't exchange with bonds, shares, silver or gold. He has chosen the "foolish things of the world to confound the wise" . . . the foolishness of child-like faith.

Those that would be rich "fall into temptation and a snare, and into many foolish and hurtful lusts, which drown men in destruction and perdition." Notice that the Scriptures say they "that will be rich;" it doesn't say that they are rich. Many are "snared" or held captive from entering into the Kingdom of God, not because they are rich, but because they desire to be. The "love of money" is the root of all evil that enslaves those who are overcome by it.

It is because of this reversal of the pecking order that the Bible tells the brother of "low degree" to rejoice because God has chosen the "poor of this world to be rich in faith." If you are fortunate enough, that as a Christian, God has allowed you to be rich, take heed to the admonition of the Word of God:

"Charge them that are rich in this world, that they be not high-minded, nor trust in uncertain riches but in the living God, who gives us richly all things to enjoy; that they do good, that they be rich in good works, ready to distribute, willing to share, laying up in store for themselves a good foundation against the time to come, that they may lay hold on eternal life."

QUOTE FOR TODAY: "Ask God to make you a David;

then ask Him where your Goliath is." - Leonard Ravenhill

* * *

TUESDAY

READING: 2 Thessalonians 3:1-18

MEMORY VERSE: "Now may the Lord direct your hearts into the love of God and into the patience of Christ." 2 Thessalonians 3:5

I am convinced that a key to victorious Christian living is the virtue of "thankfulness." He who has a truly thankful heart is producing works from faith. He who truly believes, cannot but abound with thanksgiving. He or she who believes, is thankful for God's love, thankful that his or her name is written in Heaven. Thanksgiving issues from the heart of the person who knows that all things are "working together for good to those who love God, to those who are called according to his purposes."

I remember the frustration of being a blind non-Christian. God had graciously given me a newborn baby. I wept with joy in the hospital, then jumped with thanksgiving as I left. I was so thankful, but the only trouble was, I didn't know who to thank -- I never thought of God. The minute I came to know the Lord, it was as though my blind eyes were opened to see who it was who had graciously given me life. He who is thankful for life itself will yield to the Lordship of Christ, and in doing so will be overwrought with the unspeakable gift of Calvary. It was C.H. Spurgeon who said that he is most thankful for pardon, who has felt the noose tighten around his neck. Yet, with all our material and spiritual blessings, we often lose our thankful heart the minute life slaps us in the face. Thanksgiving is relative. We don't thank God for food and children until we see pictures of starving children overseas. The old saying carries so much truth: *I used to complain I had no shoes until I met a man with no feet*. With that thought in mind consider these words from the pen of Helen Keller, the woman born blind, deaf and dumb: "For three things I thank God every day of my life: Thanks that He has vouch-safed me knowledge of His works; deep thanks that He has set in my darkness the lamp of faith; deep, deepest thanks that I have another life to look forward to -- a life joyous with light and flowers and heavenly song." Or consider these words from the famous scholar and Bible commentator, Matthew Henry, when he was accosted by thieves and robbed. He wrote the following in his diary: "Let me be thankful first, because I was never robbed before; second, because although they took my purse, they did not take my life; third, although they took my all, it was not much; and fourthly, because it was I who was robbed, not I who robbed."

QUOTE FOR TODAY: Christianity is not a pleasure

cruiser on its way to Heaven, but a lifeboat parked at the very gates of Hell.

* * *

WEDNESDAY

READING: 1 Timothy 3:1-16

MEMORY VERSE: "God was manifested in the flesh, justified in the Spirit, seen by angels, preached among the Gentiles, believed on in the world, received up into Glory." 1 Timothy 3:16

Some time ago, I was asked to visit an 18 year old girl in hospital who had attempted suicide. Tragedy had struck her family and life itself had become too much for her to bear. Even though she was a professing Christian she overdosed on sleeping pills.

As I questioned her, I found that she had traveled a predictable path. After her mother died, she found refuge in bitterness and resentment, partly against other Christians and partly against God. Bitterness, as usual, brought with it depression and that led to a suicidal tendency.

The Bible gives us a weapon against bitterness (which is a subtle tool of satan), and it is revealed in Hebrews 12:15: "Looking diligently least any of you fall short of the grace of God, least any root of bitterness springing up trouble you and by it many be defiled." The shield against bitterness is the grace of God. Grace is unmerited, undeserved, unearned favor. God has given each of us grace, and we need to show grace to those around us. Let's take a rather extreme example of grace at work. You smile at another Christian but in return you get a glare back, then a punch in the face. You are so full of grace, that instead of reacting violently, you say to yourself -- "He must be having a hard time; I must pray for him and inquire as to how I can help him." In such a situation, that sort of reaction will protect you from the poison of resentment and bitterness. If you did react in a carnal manner and say to yourself, "That so n' so, how dare he do such a thing to me. If he thinks he got away with that, he's got another thought coming! *I'll never forget what happened today!*" From then on, you harbor unforgiveness, and it will begin to fester and poison your walk with the Lord. Your bitterness won't affect the person it is aimed at. It will defile you and those who you share it with. Unforgiveness is one of satan's most subtle, and may I say, successful devices. In 2 Corinthians 2:10-11, Paul speaks of forgiveness and then says, "Least satan should get advantage of us; for we are not ignorant of his devices."

Friend, perhaps you have been ignorant of this device of satan. Perhaps you do secretly harbor unforgiveness against others and against God. Triumph through faith. No matter what has happened in the past, fall into that great safety net scripture of Romans 8:28. If you do not know what that verse is, look it up, meditate on it and claim it as your own, calling upon the grace of God to help you in your time of need.

QUOTE FOR TODAY: If you aim at the moon, you will at least clear the trees.

* * *

THURSDAY

READING: Philemon 1:1-25

MEMORY VERSE: "I thank my God, making mention of you always in my prayers, hearing of your love and faith which you have toward the Lord Jesus and toward all the saints." Philemon 1:4-5

Recently I had a short time of fellowship with a Christian brother, who not too long ago, was so into the drug

world, that his nickname was "Tony Tripper." Tony took so much L.S.D. it is a miracle that he is even able to think straight, and yet God has so healed him he is now the Pastor of a growing assembly. Other Christians from the same period of the seventies, when God's spirit touched multitudes of young people, are now thrust into the world as pastors, teachers, evangelists and missionaries. As each was scooped out of the gutter, God did what we call a "pressure cooker job." That is, He did a quick work then sent them into service of the Kingdom of God.

Such "trophies of grace," taken and used in such a short period of time, can be a source of tremendous encouragement to those who have recently come to Christ and are seeking to be used of God to reach this sick and dying world. Until that time arrives, when God opens the doors for ministry, continue to feed on the Word. Build up your inner man until he is a giant. Use the Word to chasten yourself. When you allow the Scriptures to read you as you read them, you will find things in your life which need to be purged. This is the work of the vinedresser related in John Chapter 15. If we cut the non-fruit-bearing branches off ourselves, we hasten the time of preparation. One of the greatest evangelists of all time, D.L. Moody, was tremendously influenced and challenged by these following words he heard in his younger days: "The world has yet to see what God can do . . . through a man who is fully surrendered to God." -- that man or woman can be you! Perhaps your reaction is, "Who me . . . I'm a nobody!" . . . good, *then you're God's material!* It is a principle of Scripture that God takes "the things that are not, to bring to nought the things that are." He chooses the "foolish things to confound the wise; and God has chosen the weak things of the world to confound the things which are mighty." Just change your confession by saying, "I am a nobody and that makes me God's material, here I am Lord, send me!"

QUOTE FOR TODAY: A Christian who is not filled with

the Holy Spirit and fire is like a pen with no ink. It's still a pen but if it were filled, it would make its mark more effectively.

* * *

FRIDAY

READING: Hebrews 10:1-39

MEMORY VERSE: "This is the covenant that I will make with them after those days, says the Lord: I will put My laws into their hearts, and in their minds I will write them." Hebrews 10:16

Some time ago, I was left in charge of a megaphone which our church had rented for a picnic. I returned from the Sunday night meeting to find my wife still awake, well after 11 pm, an unusual occurrence for our family. Sue related to me that she had been trying to get to sleep for some time, but had been kept awake by a number of young children who were playing on one of the neighbor's front lawns. I hit the sack, but was also somewhat hindered from stacking zzz's by those little night owls, hooting and howling.

As I lay in my bed, I suddenly remembered my weapon of warfare in the back of my car. I quickly slipped out to the garage, grabbed the megaphone, crept across the road, onto the neighbor's lawn, and up to the fence. Then, with the megaphone switched on full volume, I boldly said, *"You kids get to bed!"* I have never seen children move so fast.

I was feeling quite happy with myself until the next day,

when one of my boys related a piece of information which brought with it a hot flush to my face. One of our other female neighbors couldn't sleep because of the noise that night, and in the darkness of her kitchen was in the process of having a glass of milk. As she gazed out of the window, she saw

a sight she will never forget. A grown man dressed in pajamas, crept across her lawn, squatted in her garden, yelled through a megaphone, then ran like an exuberant little child who just did something he shouldn't, but loved it.

Although I did feel a little embarrassed when I realized that I had been seen, I did learn a valuable lesson -- there is a tremendous amount of authority in a word spoken boldly. The Bible tells Christians to "lift up your voice as a trumpet." We have the words of everlasting life to give those who will listen.

Jesus did not say to His disciples that their experience was so precious and personal that they were to keep it to themselves. He said to "shout it from the housetops." God has equipped us with more than a megaphone; He has given us His precious Holy Spirit who can take the most timid of us and make us into a roaring lion for the Kingdom of God. Such was the case with the Apostle Peter, who denied Jesus, even to a young girl.

The Holy Spirit took him and caused him to speak boldly in the name of the Lord, in the very face of the court that had taken the life of Christ and Stephen. The key to bold, fearless, effective evangelism is more than you possessing the Holy Spirit . . . it is for the Holy Spirit to possess you!

QUOTE FOR TODAY: "One distinguishing mark of an unregenerate man is ingratitude." - E. J. Conrad

* * *

SATURDAY

READING: Titus 2:1-15

MEMORY VERSE: "Who gave Himself for us, that He might redeem us from every lawless deed and purify for Himself His own special people, zealous for good works." Titus 2:14.

For over three years, I had the privilege of working in the capacity of assistant pastor. During that time, I very quickly learned my likes and dislikes. One of my dislikes was counseling "Christians" who didn't really mean business with God. Such a situation was epitomized in the following incident. A young lady sat in my office and related to me how she was being severely persecuted at her work place. She spoke, with solemn face, of how she was suffering from the attacks of the enemy and she was seeking counsel regarding leaving that job.

After twenty minutes of probing, I found out the truth of

the matter -- she didn't like working at the place . . . it had nothing to do with satan or persecution! To her, it was just another twenty minutes of self deception, to me it was twenty minutes wasted for eternity. That interview was part of a turning point in my ministry. From then on, I determined never to waste my time in that sort of counseling again. Since then God has given me one question to ask those seeking counsel, that time might be redeemed. That one question tells me whether I am using or wasting my time. Nowadays when ones seek counsel I just ask, *"Do you read the Bible each day?"* If the answer is "No," or "Sort of," or "Sometimes," I tell them, that is the root of their problem and point them to Psalm One:

"Blessed is the man who walks not in the counsel of the ungodly . . . but his delight is in the Law of the Lord; and in his Law does he meditate DAY and NIGHT."

Then the Word continues to tell us that if we do what it says we will bear fruit, our roots will be deep, we won't wither and "whatsoever" we do, it shall prosper. God gave this same promise to Joshua in Chapter 1:8 of the book of Joshua:

"This book of the Law shall not depart out of your mouth, but you shall meditate therein DAY and NIGHT . . . for then you shall make your way prosperous, and then you shall have good success."

These superficial "Christians," who are often tools of the enemy used to "wear out the saints," don't realize that all Christians have trials and temptations but because they feed on the Word continually, they are strong enough to stand tall in the storms. They don't run for counsel every time a trial comes because they are grounded in the principles of the Word of God. They rejoice in tribulation knowing that it can only "establish, strengthen and settle them;" they continue in the Word, being "disciples indeed; they know the truth and the truth has made them free."

QUOTE FOR TODAY: Following the paths of least resistance is what makes rivers and men crooked.

* * *

SUNDAY

READING: 2 Timothy 4:1-22

MEMORY VERSE: "But you be watchful in all things, endure afflictions, do the work of an evangelist, fulfill your ministry." 2 Timothy 4:5

I'm sure it is the general experience of newly converted Christians to almost panic when the realization comes that they have family and friends who are not saved. After

banging one's head against the brick wall of self-righteousness or so-called atheism, one is forced to one's knees to pray a pleading, panic-filled prayer. This doesn't need to be so. Often our tearful pleadings are just an outward sign of a hard heart of unbelief. If we truly trust in God we will completely relax in His promises.

If we want to see our loved ones come to a knowledge of salvation, we must learn to pray effectively. Firstly, let's establish a basis for our faith; -- is it God's will for your family and friends to be saved? The answer is abundantly clear from 2 Peter 3:9. "(God) is not willing that any should perish but that all should come to repentance." It is God's will for your family to be saved, therefore you can pray a believing, confident, faith-filled prayer. In Mark 11:22-24 Jesus said, "Have faith in God. For assuredly, I say to you, whoever says to this mountain, be removed and cast into the sea, and does not doubt in his heart, but believes that those things he says will come to pass, he will have whatever he says. Therefore I say to you, whatever things you ask when you pray, believe that you receive them, and you will have them." Instead of imagining your loved ones dying in their sins, see them in your mind as Christ-centered on-fire Christians, and begin thanking God in faith. Say, "Thank you Lord, that You are not willing my family perish, so I know I'm praying your will. Thank you Lord that they will soon be Christians because You have said if I ask believing I shall receive." This type of believing prayer will have the effect of ridding your heart of the weight of worry -- cast all your care on the Lord. Show you believe by rejoicing now! Faith calls "those things which are not as though they were." Look at the thanksgiving and confidence Jesus had in John Chapter 11 before He raised Lazarus from the grave. "Father, I thank You that You have heard Me." Thanksgiving for answered prayer before it is answered is true faith. In fact, it is the norm for all who want to see results. Philippians 4:6-7 says, "Be anxious for nothing, but in everything by prayer and supplication, with thanksgiving, let your requests be made known to God; and the peace of God, which surpasses all understanding, will guard your hearts and minds through Christ Jesus."

QUOTE FOR TODAY: We have sought to make the Gospel acceptable to men, rather than men acceptable.

* * *

MONDAY

READING: James 1:1-27

MEMORY VERSE: "Instead you ought to say, If the Lord wills, we shall live and do this or that." James 4:15.

Recently, a very angry man in his late thirties burst from a crowd to which I was speaking in an open-air meeting and screamed at the top of his voice, "You and your God are responsible for busting up my family!" From what I could make out, his two daughters had just become Christians and had, for some reason, left home. Their conversion had nothing to do with me, but this gentleman seemed to feel that I was directly responsible to a point where he was close to

rearranging my facial features. Quite frankly, I felt sorry for him and pointed out that the answer to his plight was in his own hands. I told him that he should become a Christian. This seemed too much for him to handle. He became so consumed with anger that he stormed out of the crowd, but couldn't leave without letting off more steam. He did a U-turn and came back into the crowd with so much anger, an elderly gentleman, in fairly colorful language, told him that he was making a fool of himself. This time he stormed off still in a rage.

A week later, when I had finished speaking, I was approached by that same man, but this time his facial expression was different. With tears in his eyes, he apologized for his behavior and related to me how he had become a Christian. God had forgiven him and healed him of an alcohol problem! During that brief conversation, he related something to me which was so refreshing to hear in these days of self-righteousness. He said, "I was blaming God, when it wasn't God's fault but mine."

In that penitent Psalm of David, Psalm 51, notice how David admits his guilt. Look where he puts the blame, " . . . blot out my transgressions. Wash me thoroughly from my iniquity, and cleanse me from my sin. For I acknowledge my transgressions, and my sin is ever before me."

Sadly, it took the sobering rebuke of Nathan the prophet to awaken David to his state before God. In sinning with Bathsheba, his heart had become hardened by the "deceitfulness of sin."

Friend, perhaps you have been blaming everyone but yourself for your plight. Be honest with yourself, acknowledge your sin to God and ask for mercy and cleansing before the Day of Judgment. "He that covers his sins shall not prosper, but whoever confesses and forsakes them shall have mercy."

QUOTE FOR TODAY: "In our prayer time, there ought to be, on our part, a deep desire to have a conscience void of offense toward God and men." - Paris Reidhead

* * *

TUESDAY

READING: James 2:1-26

MEMORY VERSE: "For as the body without the spirit is dead, so faith without works is dead also." James 2:26

I find preaching the Gospel to the unsaved both a privilege and a challenge. One of the greatest challenges of

my ministry presented itself recently, when I was invited to speak at a large university. This was my second visit to the university, the first being somewhat disappointing. I had spoken to about 80 or so students and had perceived an apathy among them which I was unable to penetrate. This time I arrived to be told that the Christian students had flooded the campus with 2,000 copies of our publication called Living Waters. This issue dealt with abortion, homosexuality, rock music and the occult, with a full-page gentle word from Jesus, "Except you repent, you shall perish." I was told that the paper had made the students extremely angry; in fact, they had actually been tearing up posters advertising my visit.

About ten minutes before I was due to speak, I was shown a letter written by the University Chaplain which was displayed on the main notice board. It read something like this, "I would like it to be known that I have had nothing at all to do with the inviting of Ray Comfort to this university. I disagree with his message. I believe he will put students off real Christianity."

Then he listed 7 or 8 points of contention between his message and mine. I must admit I felt rather discouraged, but I had forgotten something important about rebellious, disobedient human nature. Tell most people not to do something, and they may just do the opposite. Such was the case with the students. Five hundred beansprout-eating, peace-marching, pro-abortionistic, homosexual, dope-smoking, health-freak, fire-spitting radicals filled that hall. *Every seat was taken . . . it was incredible.*

The next day 800 sardined students squeezed into the hall for 45 minutes and hated every word I spoke. I have never in my life seen such unified, blasphemous, foul-mouthed, hatred directed at the Gospel.

These are our future doctors, lawyers and politicians. But where sin abounds, there does much more grace abound -- it was an opportunity I wouldn't have missed for the world.

In fact, I recommend that every preacher has an ungodly University Chaplain go before him and prepare the way with nasty letters to ensure the success of his ministry!

QUOTE FOR TODAY: "Our hatred of someone does not affect their peace of mind, but it certainly can ruin ours." - W. A. Nance

* * *

WEDNESDAY

READING: 2 Peter 2:1-22

MEMORY VERSE: "These are wells without water, clouds carried by a tempest, to whom the gloom of darkness is reserved forever." 2 Peter 2:17

I am so pleased the Bible tells us that there is an anger

that you and I can have, without sinning. It says, "be angry and sin not." Jesus was angered, without sin, when He cleared the temple of the sacrilegious moneychangers.

There are many things in today's society which cause my blood to boil -- dead, dry religion, which masquerades as God's representation on earth; so called peace marchers who seek peace, without God; anti-Christian music which is hardening our youth against the Gospel of salvation, and many other things too numerous to list. But that which I desire to bring to your attention is one pet hatred I have. It is the continual glory the world gives to 'Mother Nature.' One hears often the words, "Look how wonderfully 'Mother Nature' has done this or that." Praise is heaped upon the "creature," rather than the "Creator."

Imagine for a moment, a program on world art. A brilliant painter is actually on hand, as his art is being displayed. How unthinkable it would be for a television commentator to push aside the brilliant artist, then draw the attention of the television audience to the painting with the  words, "Look how 'brother paint' has found its way onto the canvas. Notice the beautiful lines across the face, the expression in the eyes. The stroke of 'mother brush' has been so brilliantly portrayed onto this canvas."

No, it would be unthinkable that the veneration be given

to the paint, but the painter. It is an expression of his genius.

The more brilliant the painter, the more of a crime it is to ignore him and give the glory to another, especially when the other is non-existent.

How it grieves me to hear the world give the glory due to our God, to creation. The genius of God's marvelous hand is so clearly evidently ignored. How true are the words of Job:

"Lo these are parts of his ways; but how little a portion is heard of Him."

The Apostle Paul tells us in Romans Chapter 1, that such foolishness has been around since sin found its way into the heart of man. Speaking of an ancient reprobate Roman civilization, he says, "(They) changed the truth of God for a lie, and worshipped and served the creature, more than the Creator, who is blessed forever. Amen."

QUOTE FOR TODAY: In Catholicism, evangelical zeal is diffused by purgatory, in Protestantism, by apathy.

* * *

THURSDAY

READING: John 4:1-26

MEMORY VERSE: "God is Spirit, and those who worship Him must worship in spirit and truth." John 4:24

Most Christians feel stirred to pray for revival. And so they should, but there is something each of us must understand. First, we must know what we mean by "revival." It doesn't just mean a temporal stirring of the local church for a week or so. It means a complete overhaul of the Church to a point where we see the world transformed by God through His Body on earth. Yet, here is the subtlety of the enemy: he has convinced many within the  Body of Christ, that revival is so in the category of the sovereignty of God, that all we can do is "pray it in." That seems spiritual, but on closer examination, those who are of the opinion that all we can do to affect a revival is pray, are saying that God will save the lost without any evangelical effort on the part of the Church. Its prayer is:

"God save sinners. Send revival. Forget the fact that Your Word says, 'How shall they hear without a preacher?' and 'God has chosen the foolishness of PREACHING to save them that believe,' and 'The Gospel is the power of God to salvation.' God, YOU preach the Gospel to every creature, we commit the word of reconciliation back into Your hands . . . we will stay inside and pray for revival while You do the task You have ensigned to us."

God will not circumnavigate His means of salvation of the lost. The fact is, the ones in the Church praying for revival, yet not being witnesses, are the very ones who need reviving. When the Church preaches to the lost, then God blesses His Word and uses the foolishness of preaching to save them that believe. That is the Divine plan for the salvation of sinners and no amount of prayer without obedience to the Great Commission will get the job done.

When Paul asked for prayer while he was in chains in the Philippian jail, he neither asked prayer for his release, nor did he ask those to whom he was writing to pray for the salvation of those in the jail.

What he asked for, was prayer that he would be bold in his witness; that he would open his mouth boldly and speak as he ought to. Let's follow his example.

QUOTE FOR TODAY: "The history of man is his attempt to escape his own corruption." - Daniel Mullis

* * *

FRIDAY

READING: John 10:1-21

MEMORY VERSE: "The thief comes not but to steal, and to kill, and to destroy; I have come that they might have life, and that they might have it more abundantly." John 10:10

There was once an alcoholic who, like many alcoholics, found himself without a friend in the world. The only companion he did have was a mangy old dog. The dog was a faithful old friend. He would sit for hours at his master's feet waiting for him to come to, after each of his drinking bouts.

One night, the alcoholic staggered home and crashed onto the living room floor. The old dog faithfully laid at his feet as usual. For some reason, during the early hours of the morning, the dog began to bark incessantly. The

alcoholic stirred from his drunken stupor. The last thing he felt like, in the condition he was in, was listening to a barking dog.

As he lay there, the noise of the bark seemed to echo in his mind. He staggered to his feet and in a blind rage, threw a chair at the old dog whose bark seemed bigger than his bone-brain.

Some hours later, he awoke to find himself back on the floor and to his dismay, thieves had entered his home during the night and stripped it of every movable object. Then, with tear-filled eyes, he stared in unbelief at the only two remaining objects; one was a broken chair, the other . . . a dead dog lying beneath it. In his drunken rage he had killed that faithful companion who was only trying to warn him of thieves who were breaking into his home.

Each of us has a faithful old companion who seeks to

warn us of the thieves who break into our home and strip it of things of true value. That old friend is called "conscience." He seems to bark at the most annoying times.

There are times when we would like to cry out, "Oh, to be free from the cries of conscience!" There are even some, who in blind rage, kill that faithful protector of the home. The Bible warns that men will have consciences which are "seared with a hot iron." In other words, there is no life left in their conscience -- there is no bark when the thief comes to "kill, steal and destroy" (John 10:10). Let's not throw the chair at our old companion, but let us as the Scriptures exhort:

"Be sober," -- be alert, not only to the fact of the thief who seeks to rob us, but to keep our conscience tender with a ready ear to hear when the warning cry comes.

QUOTE FOR TODAY: Great minds discuss ideas, average minds discuss events, small minds discuss people.

* * *

SATURDAY

READING: Romans 1:1-32

MEMORY VERSE: "For the wrath of God is revealed from Heaven against all ungodliness and unrighteousness of men, who hold the truth in unrighteousness." Romans 1:18

In the closing of this age, many Christians find themselves confronted with "enlightened" pseudo-intellectuals who take great delight and security in stockading themselves behind a pile of arguments against Christianity. We have those who make monkeys of themselves by blind faith in the religion of science. Others believe we were placed here by supernatural creatures from outer space, while still others

have beliefs as far-fetched as the imagination can stretch.

The truth of the matter is that they prefer to believe a lie rather than accept the truth. The truth about God brings with it a responsibility the ungodly would rather do without. Their ignorance is wilful. It is because of wilful ignorance, they grope around in their dark imaginations, refusing to flick the switch which is within easy reach of each of them (Romans 10:8).

Such was the case with the "rationalists" of the time of Christ, the Sadducees. These people refused to accept anything that didn't have a rational explanation. They were advocates of the theory of annihilation; i.e. they didn't believe in life after death, which explains why they were sad, you see. These brains of humanity approached Jesus with what they thought was the ultimate stumper of questions. In fact, it sounds more like a plot to a Disney movie:

"Then came to Him certain of the Sadducees, who deny that there is any resurrection; and they asked Him, saying, master, Moses wrote to us, If any man's brother die, having a wife, and he die without children, that his brother should take his wife, and raise up seed unto his brother. There were, therefore, seven brethren; and the first took a wife, and died without children.

And the second took her as his wife, and he died childless. And the third took her; and in the same manner the seven also; and they left no children, and died. Last of all the woman died also. Therefore, in the resurrection whose wife of them is she? For seven had her as wife" (Luke 20:27-33).

If you read the passage yourself, you will see that it was no stumper for the Son of God. The narrative is just another example of the love of God, in that Jesus condescended to answer a pathetic question from another skeptic and ignorant darkened soul.

QUOTE FOR TODAY: "Anyone who angers you, conquers you." - Sister Kenny

* * *

SUNDAY

READING: Luke 11:33-54

MEMORY VERSE: "Take heed, therefore, that the light which is in you is not darkness." Luke 11:35

Most of us are on our best behavior when we are guests at someone's home, but I can imagine the regret in the heart of one red-faced Pharisee, who asked Jesus to dine with him. The Pharisee marvelled that Jesus hadn't gone through the usual religious observances in washing before dinner.

That was all Jesus needed. Then came powerful, convicting words from the Son of God:

"Now do you Pharisees make clean the outside of the cup and the platter; but your inward part is full of ravening and wickedness. You fools, did not He that made that which is without make that which is within also? But rather give alms of such things as you have; and, behold, all things are clean to you. But woe to you, Pharisees! for you tithe mint and rue and all manner of herbs, and pass over judgment and the love of God; these ought you to have done, and not to leave the other undone. Woe to you, Pharisees! for you love the uppermost seats in the synagogues, and greetings in the markets. Woe to you, Scribes and Pharisees, hypocrites! for you are as graves which appear not, and men that walk over them are not aware of them."

Jesus doesn't eat when He has something to say. When you became a Christian, you invited Him to come and dine with you (Revelation 3:20), what is He saying to you at the moment? Is He leaning back and enjoying an intimate dinner with you, or is He saying "Hypocrite!" If He is putting His holy finger on something which is displeasing to Him, get it right with Him now, don't put it off another second. You see, Jesus loved those hypocritical Pharisees enough to rebuke them. If He didn't, He wouldn't have bothered even speaking to them about their sins and let them tumble into Hell. That's why we need to listen for the rebukes, because His rebuke this side of Judgment Day is motivated by love and concern for us so that we might be pure, and free from His wrath on that Great and Terrible Day of The Lord.

QUOTE FOR TODAY: Reckon him a Christian indeed who is not ashamed of the Gospel, nor a shame to it.

* * *

MONDAY

READING: Philippians 2:1-30

MEMORY VERSE: "Look not every man on his own things, but every man also on the things of others." Philippians 2:4

Actor W.C. Fields was so afraid of losing his loose cash he opened bank accounts whenever he found himself with coins in his pocket. Among the pseudonyms he used were: Figley E. Whitesides, Aristotle Hoop, Ludovic Fishpond, and Cholmondley Frampton-Blythe. There are literally hundreds of these accounts with different names and as a master list was never made, they will never be closed.

What's in a name anyway. The only reason we have a name is so that we can be distinguished from each other. However, God puts far more emphasis on names than we do. In fact, there are many incidents where God changed the name of men and women to signify something special.

For example, God changed Abram's name, which means "exalted father," to Abraham, meaning "father of a multitude". Sarai also had her name changed to Sarah, which means "princess." Jacob was changed to Israel, which means "he who strives with God," while other well-known Biblical

name changes are Simon to Peter and Saul to Paul. Each has a hidden significance, but the most significant name meaning in Scripture, is that of Jesus.

When the Angel of the Lord said to Mary, "And, behold, you shall conceive in your womb, and bring forth a son, and you shall call his name Jesus," the name came from a Greek word "Lesous" and is a transliteration of the Hebrew word "Joshua," which means "Jehovah is Salvation," i.e. Jehovah is the Savior. This name is tremendously significant in that it reaffirms the most comprehensive of Bible doctrines, the deity of Jesus Christ.

It is interesting to note that in the Epistle of James, Peter, John and Jude, men who accompanied Jesus, He is referred to as "Jesus Christ," as that was the order of their experience. They knew Him as "Jesus," the Savior, and afterward, they believed on Him as the "Christ," the Messiah. But the Apostle Paul came to know Him in the reverse order. His experience was coming to know Him in His glorified state first, which may be why Paul often refers to the Lord as "Christ Jesus." In his letters, the use of the name is always in harmony with the context, such as Philippians 2:5, when "Christ Jesus" describes the exalted One Who emptied Himself for our redemption. For those who know him as the Christ and Savior, His name is "wonderful."

QUOTE FOR TODAY: He who pulls on the oars, hasn't time to rock the boat.

* * *

TUESDAY

READING: Luke 24:13-32

MEMORY VERSE: "Did not our hearts burn within us, while He talked with us along the way, and while He opened to us the Scriptures?" Luke 24:32

I'm sure most Christians have come up against those who say, "If God wants to save me, He will in His own good time." Even in Christian circles there are those who say that if God wants to fill them with the Holy Spirit, He will do so in His own good time. Yet, often God puts the onus on us. The Bible is full of exhortations to "seek the

Lord," "desire earnestly," "ask," "knock," "call," and many others. Usually God (in His grace) requires that we take the initiative and exercise faith in His promises.

In Mark we read: "And when evening was come, the ship was in the midst of the sea, and He alone on the land. And He saw them toiling in rowing; for the wind was contrary unto them: and about the fourth watch of the night He came to them, walking upon the sea, and would have passed by them. But when they saw Him walking upon the sea, they supposed it had been a spirit, and cried out: for they all saw Him, and were troubled. And immediately He talked with them, and said to them, Be of good cheer: it is I, be not afraid."

Notice the Bible says that Jesus would have passed by the disciples, but He heeded their cry. The same thing happened on the road to Emmaus -- "And beginning at Moses and all the prophets, He expounded to them in the Scriptures the things concerning Himself. Then they drew near to the village where they were going, and He indicated that He would have gone farther. But they constrained Him, saying, 'Abide with us, for it is toward evening, and the day is far spent.' And He went in to stay with them." The word "constrain" means "to urge with power sufficient to produce the effect." In other words, the disciples wanted

Jesus with them and they wouldn't take "No" for an answer -- they wanted Him to stay.

God is pleased when we want His presence with us. Never let the Lord pass you by in any area of your life. Constrain Him to spend time with you; that's the essence of a good relationship.

QUOTE FOR TODAY: We shouldn't follow after signs and wonders; they should follow us.

* * *

WEDNESDAY

READING: Proverbs 3:1-35

MEMORY VERSE: "Happy is the man who finds wisdom and the man who gains understanding." Proverbs 3:13

Some time ago, I approached a rather large "bikie" whose motorbike had broken down. I asked him if I could be of any help to him and was pleased to find that I could, first by allowing him to use my office phone, then by giving him a ride home in my car.

A year or so later, I was greatly encouraged to find that he had become a Christian. God had got hold of him and made him a new creature in Christ.

It was only then that I found out that the day I approached him, he had turned around from his bike, totally frustrated about his situation and was fully intending to beat me to a pulp.

But it seems there was Divine intervention; either that or

one look at me had made him change his mind.

As the months passed, this new Christian began to grow in grace, then something happened which showed once again that Christians are not immune to the storms of life. My friend was working at a wool store lifting bales

of wool using steel hooks, when a hook ripped from one of the bales and went straight into his left eye. His reaction was quite natural. He cried out, *"Where are you God when I need you!"* sprinkled with one or two very colorful curse words.

Suddenly, the peace of God enveloped him. Aware of God's presence, he said, "I'm sorry Lord . . . please forgive me." Then he was rushed to hospital. His attitude was so radically different from what you would expect, his co-workers were taken back. In fact, a nurse who was with this young man told me that other doctors and nurses couldn't get over the fact that he was so polite, seeing that he came from such an obviously hardened background.

His eye was removed and replaced with an artificial one which, I must admit, was hardly distinguishable from the other eye.

One cannot help feeling humbled by the whole incident. His reaction was admirable. I'm sure many a professing Christian would weaken and ask the question, "Why did

God let this happen to me?" Yet, the following are his words, "Before I was a Christian, I had two eyes yet I was blind. Now I have only one eye, *but I can see all things clearly.*"

QUOTE FOR TODAY: "The Bible suffers more from its exponents than its opponents." C.H. Spurgeon

* * *

THURSDAY

READING: Luke 9:1-27

MEMORY VERSE: "Then He said to them all, if anyone desires to come after Me, let him deny himself, and take up his cross daily, and follow Me." Luke 9:23

There are a number of things in life that make me really angry. One of these is cigarette advertising. The Bible tells us we are like sheep, and coming from a country where there are twenty sheep to every person, I can appreciate the analogy. Sheep are easily led. In fact, a "Judas" sheep is commonly used to lead the sheep to the slaughter.

The smoking industry is the ultimate Judas sheep. A number of years ago, greedy wolves in sheep's clothing decided to target women as potential customers for their filthy habit, so they exploited the fact that today's woman longs to be slim. They deliberately used ultra slim women in their advertising, then enhanced the photos to exaggerate their sleek shape and even make them look anorexic. The cigarettes themselves were made slimmer, the brand name contained the word "slim," and even wording type in the advertisement was slim.

Others exploited the fact that women often suffer from stress. They emphasized some stressful situation and placed a woman in the middle of the advertisement, lying on a beach chair while smoking a cigarette. Others used the word "choice" and pictured groups of "liberated" women laughing together, each clutching a cigarette.

Well, it has worked; sales sky-rocketed. In Kentucky, one out of every three women smoke cigarettes, while other states aren't too far behind. Incidents of lung cancer have also sky-rocketed. In recent years, it has overtaken all other forms of cancer and become number one of the cancer killing diseases. Can you imagine what it would be like to get lung cancer; to have the very organs which draw air into your body, actually rot, so that every breath you take, day and night, carries with it a terrifying panic? Experiment for a moment. Close your mouth, then pinch your nose so that just the bare minimum of air can get through your nostrils. Do that for sixty seconds (don't cheat), and get a taste of what it must be like for those unsuspecting poor souls who are the victims of the cigarette industry. If you smoke, stop. If you don't smoke, never put one to your mouth. Respect the body God has entrusted you with; and pray for the salvation of those who are responsible for cigarette advertising. May God in His great mercy, grant them repentance, because I wouldn't be in their shoes on Judgment Day for all the tea in China.

QUOTE FOR TODAY: "Never be afraid to trust an unknown future to a known God." - Corrie Ten Boom

* * *

FRIDAY

READING: Acts 3:1-26

MEMORY VERSE: "Repent, therefore, and be converted, that your sins may be blotted out." Acts 3:19

I'm sure if you have read some of the words of David in Psalms (especially in reference to his enemies), you will have found it difficult to reconcile with New Testament teaching. For example he said things like, "All nations compassed me about; but in the name of the Lord will I destroy them."

However, it isn't difficult to see the spiritual application.

Humanity is surrounded by "principalities and powers,

spiritual wickedness in high places." These fallen spirits are both enemies of God and of the Church; we are continually in a spiritual battle.

As the enemy comes against us, we can have victory through the "name of the Lord." This victory isn't confined to the Old Testament; Jesus said, "In MY NAME shall they cast out devils." Demons tremble at His name because God "has given Him a name which is above every name." So whatever you do, do it in the name of Jesus, whether it is preaching (Luke 24:27), praying (John 14:13), healing the sick (Acts 3:6), giving thanks (Ephesians 5:20), or gathering together (Colossians 3:17).

Why does the Bible put so much emphasis on the name of Jesus? It is because the name of Jesus is the Key to unlock all the promises of God (2 Corinthians 1:20).

When we stand, preach or pray in the name of Jesus, we can have the utmost confidence that God will (according to His good pleasure) appropriate every promise He has made. In Christ I have the King's approval; I am His and He is mine. I have been adopted into His family and have consequently inherited His wonderful name and all that goes with it. That's why the enemy flees.

Obviously, we are not to use the name of Jesus as some sort of magical chant, but as long as we keep our lives free of sin, trusting in God's mercy, walking according to His Word, we can have the confidence that God is with us, and we are "more than conquerors through Him that loved us."

QUOTE FOR TODAY: "Hot heads and cold hearts never solved anything." - Billy Graham

* * *

SATURDAY

READING: Ephesians 6:1-24

MEMORY VERSE: "Put on the whole armor of God, that you may be able to stand against the wiles of the devil." Ephesians 6:11

The next time you feel fear come upon you, open your Bible at Psalm 56. In this Psalm, as in many other places,

the Scriptures give the answer to fear. The Psalmist begins by casting his care (anxiety) upon the Lord, then confessing victory -- "Whenever I am afraid, I will trust in you." Notice that he doesn't deny the reality of his fears, but says when it comes, he will deal with it by trusting in God. He then produces for us another key -- the power of praise (verse 10). We can see this in action when Paul and Silas were cast into prison for their faith. No doubt they were fearful, yet they found victory through faith which expressed itself through praise.

Faith is a command of Scripture. Jesus said, "Have faith in God." So to fail to walk in faith is not only to disobey the Word of God, but it is to leave ourselves in the realm of tormenting fear. The Bible likens faith to a shield which will quench all the fiery darts of the enemy.

Fear is one of satan's chief darts. It can turn a potentially great man or great woman of God into a quivering, faithless, slave of fear.

At the end of this age, more than ever before, you and I must learn how to overcome fears because Jesus spoke of fear as being one of the signs of the end times.

The world will have many hearts that will fail because of fear, but you and I are not of this world. Whatever comes our way can be dwarfed through faith. Mountains can be cast into the sea of God's wonderful promises.

Remember the example set for us by Stephen, the first one to die for faith in Jesus. He was a person just like you and me; he had pains and fear but he looked above the pounding rocks of man's hatred for God, looking to Jesus, the author and finisher of our faith, who for the joy that was set before Him, endured the cross, despising the shame and is seated at the right hand of God.

But notice what happened when Stephen saw Jesus -- he saw Him standing at the right hand of the Father. What a salute, what a welcome, what concern for His beloved martyr.

So the next time fear comes knocking at your door, peep over the top of your shield of faith just long enough to hit him in the face with the sword of the Word . . . he won't hang around too long.

QUOTE FOR TODAY: God is searching for the smallest people to do the greatest thing.

* * *

SUNDAY

READING: Psalm 66

MEMORY VERSE: "Blessed be God, who has not turned away my prayer, nor His mercy from me." Psalm 66:20

God's Word is like a light. Our closeness to the light is determined not by distance, but by the faith which we exercise when reading it. We can read God's Word intently but without faith being added, the light of the Word won't shine upon our hearts.

Unless we believe what we read and receive it into a "good and honest heart" it will fall on dead ground . . . it won't bring life.

With this thought in mind, let's allow the light of God's Word to search our hearts with the following Scripture:

"And He has made my mouth like a sharp sword; in the shadow of His hand has He hid me, and made me a polished shaft; in His quiver has He hid me" (Isaiah 49:2).

We can begin by asking ourselves: "Has God made my mouth like a sharp sword?"

This is an clear and wonderful picture of expressing

God's Word. It doesn't mean that we speak continually in King James English or we go about quoting Scripture to everyone we see, but it means that we allow the Word of Christ to dwell richly within our hearts. We speak the Word to the storm. The Bible says of Jesus, "Out of His mouth went a sharp two-edged sword" (Revelation 1:16).

This Scripture also reminds us of the Divine protection of God, "In the shadow of His hand has He hid me." When we become Christians, God puts His "everlasting arms underneath and around about us." Jesus said that no man shall pluck us out of the hand of God. The only way we can be in a shadow while in God's hand is for His hand to come between us and the sun. The sun is a type of tribulation, temptation and persecution (Mark 4:17, Matthew 13:21, Luke 8:13). As the fiery heat of tribulation beats down upon us, God knows just when to bring His loving hand across to shield us from its burning rays.

According to this verse, we should be a polished shaft or arrow, hidden in His quiver. It is rather painful to place the arrow, pull back the bow and fire, and feel a splinter pierce the soft flesh at the base of your thumb and forefinger. God wants to launch us as a polished arrow in the direction of His choosing without resistance. To do this He must polish us . . . often called a "sandpaper ministry." God will chasten us, refine us and cleanse us through adversity making us useful in His service.

"So whoever cleanses himself (from what is ignoble and unclean), who separates himself from contact with contaminating and corrupting influences -- will then himself be a vessel separate and useful for honorable and noble purposes, consecrated and profitable to the Master, fit and ready for any good work" (2 Timothy 2:21 Amplified Bible).

QUOTE FOR TODAY: A smile is an asset, a frown is a liability.

* * *

MONDAY

READING: 2 Timothy 2:1-26

MEMORY VERSE: "Study to show yourself approved unto God, a workman that needs not to be ashamed, rightly dividing the Word of truth." 2 Timothy 2:15

Stephen was a man who proved himself in God -- a man full of faith and of the Holy Ghost. The last hours of Stephen's life should challenge each of us as to how committed we are to Jesus.

When Stephen was reviled and persecuted for the Gospel's sake the Bible says his face shone with the Glory of God. I wonder how each of us stands up to persecution? Do we get angry or impatient or does the joy and love of God become evident on our face?

When Stephen stood up to give defense against his accusers he revealed that he was a man who knew and used the Scriptures. He revealed that, like Jesus, he feared no man. He was bold in his God. Each of us should be challenged by this portion of Scripture. Stephen knew the punishment for so-called blasphemy and yet he refused to deny his Lord.

In the book of Revelation, Jesus commends those who followed Stephen and laid down their lives for the faith:

"And they overcame him by the blood of the Lamb, and by the word of their testimony; and they loved not their lives unto the death" (Revelation 12:11).

In most countries we would have to try very hard indeed to be persecuted physically for being a Christian. But Stephen in the face of such hostility "reviled not." Paul tells us how we should react against those that oppose themselves: "And the servant of the Lord must not strive; but be gentle unto all men, able to teach, patient, in meekness instructing those that oppose themselves; if God peradventure will give them repentance to the acknowledging of the truth; and that they may recover themselves out of the snare of the devil, who are taken captive by him at his will" (2 Timothy 2:24-26). Stephen, under the most severe tests revealed what was actually in his heart, "And they stoned Stephen, calling upon God, and saying, Lord Jesus, receive my spirit. And he kneeled down, and cried with a loud voice, Lord, lay not this sin to their charge. And when he had said this, he fell asleep" (Acts 7:59-60).

QUOTE FOR TODAY: When you meet temptation, turn to the right.

* * *

TUESDAY

READING: Psalm 68

MEMORY VERSE: "Let God arise, let His enemies be scattered; let those also who hate Him flee before Him." Psalm 68:1

How each of us longs for the power we see demonstrated in the book of Acts -- to see people being healed of diseases by the very shadow cast by Christians. In today's Scripture we have the key to power within the life of the believer " . . . declared to be the Son of God with power, according to the spirit of holiness by the resurrection from the dead." If we want to move in the realm of the power of God, we need to understand the meaning of the word holiness so we might see the result of holiness. The ultimate result of holiness is resurrection. If Jesus hadn't been holy, the virtue of God would not have been manifest through Him. If we want to be part of the first resurrection we must "be holy even as God is Holy" (Numbers 15:40-41).

Holiness means to be separated. Holiness, repentance and sanctification go hand in hand and are collectively the keys to moving in the miracle realm. Demons know this, even if we don't: "And there was in their synagogue a man with an unclean spirit; and he cried out saying, Let us alone; what have we to do with Thee, Jesus of Nazareth? Have you come to destroy us? I know who you are, the Holy One of God" (Mark 1:23-24). Demons are fearful of holiness because they know of the power which accompanies it!

In reality, to have the "spirit of holiness" means to have

the Holy Spirit and to let the Holy Spirit have you. Being "separated" doesn't mean to cut yourself off from those around you, those you are seeking to reach for the Gospel; but it means to cut yourself off from their works. Ephesians 5:17 says,

"Wherefore be not un-wise, but understanding what the will of the Lord is."

If you don't know God's will for your life, you are unwise! The Bible clearly says, "This is the will of God even your sanctification" (1 Thessalonians 4:3). Sanctification is "the progressive conformation of the believer into the image of Christ, or the process by which the life is made morally holy."

If we want God to move in our lives in power, we must see the need to look to Jesus and follow His example of "holiness unto the Lord," that we might be declared to be a child of God with power, according to the spirit of holiness.

QUOTE FOR TODAY: "The greatest waste in the world is the difference between what we are and what we could be." - Ben Herbster

* * *

WEDNESDAY

READING: 1 John 2:1-29

MEMORY VERSE: "Do not love the world or the things in the world. If anyone loves the world, the love of the Father is not in him." 1 John 2:15

Some time ago I prayed a very dangerous prayer. I asked the Lord to allow incidents to happen in my life which I could use as sermon illustrations. God has so honored that prayer that I am somewhat apprehensive to begin each day.

One incident that comes to mind is an invitation I had to speak at a Sunday evening service at a New Life Center in the local suburb of Halswell, New Zealand -- I had been given the directions to find the hall in which they met.

On the Sunday night at about 6:50 pm, I was driving along Halswell Road when I saw lights on in a building and cars parked outside. As I entered, I glanced into the room to make sure it wasn't a service group or scout meeting. A group of people were obviously readying themselves for the service, with one young man putting transparencies on an overhead projector for the singing. It was obviously the right place. I then looked for the pre-service prayer meeting. It was being held in a back room. I quietly joined in with a feeling of excitement as these dear saints sought God's anointing on the meeting. At seven o'clock one brother committed the service to the Lord, then closed in prayer. Suddenly, all eyes were on me!? I greeted them, then asked, "New Life Center Halswell?" and received the startling reply, "No, Saint Luke's!" It turned out that New Life Center was two hundred yards down the road -- *I was at the wrong church!*

Three days later, I was in another city staying in a block of apartments with some friends. At 10:30 that evening I arrived "home" somewhat exhausted after the meeting. My friend had kindly left the back door unlocked and the light was on to illuminate my path.

I opened the door, then carefully locked it on the inside and made my way to the bathroom. I stood there in shock that they were able to renovate that bathroom in such a short time. Then it struck me -- *I was in the wrong apartment!* I sneaked down the hall, unbolted the back door and slipped out, somewhat embarrassed.

In both incidents, I "seemed" to be on the right track. The Bible says,

"There is a way which seems right to man but the end thereof is death."

That is why the Scriptures implore us to make our "calling and election sure."

Friend, if you are not trusting in Jesus alone for your salvation, the path you are walking may seem right, but it ends in eternal damnation -- and if you do find yourself in the wrong place after death, there won't be any back door to slip out and make right your error.

QUOTE FOR TODAY: I'd rather walk barefoot to Heaven, than ride a cadillac to Hell.

* * *

THURSDAY

READING: Jude 1:1-25

MEMORY VERSE: "But others save with fear, pulling them out of the fire, hating even the garment defiled by the flesh." - Jude 1:23

Several years ago my daughter, much to my delight,  sought my expertise with the words, "Dad, what color do you think I should do the wording on my school project?" With many years of experience in designing literature, I related how I felt that the most outstanding colors, in my opinion, were yellow with a black border. I suggested yellow. The reply came -- "What about green?" I thought to myself, "Well, she doesn't want yellow," so I suggested red as the next most outstanding color. The reply came, "What about green?" I breathed a deep sigh and said, "Green then." There was then a delighted "Thanks Dad," and off she went.

This somewhat amusing incident came right in the middle of when I had been praying about making an important decision to move from one assembly to another. I saw how clearly you and I can deceive ourselves. There is something we want, so we make it a "matter of prayer." Instead of seeking the advice of God we actually pray about it just to appease our conscience, then do what we wanted to do anyway. We "acknowledge Him in all our ways," then we bring it to pass.

In Psalm 106, we see this clearly illustrated with Israel. The Psalmist relates God's goodness to Israel and His great works of deliverance on their behalf. But it says of that generation, "They soon forgot His works; they waited not for His counsel, but lusted exceedingly in the wilderness, and tempted God in the desert. And He gave them their request, but sent leanness into their soul."

In the past I have learned that it pays to wait on the Lord for His direction. Many a time I have prayed, just to appease my conscience and ended up making a wrong decision. I feel so sorry for some Christians who are seeking a marriage partner. They tell God what they are going to do in the guise of a request, then realize in time their foolishness. It does well in regard to prayer, to take heed to the words of James to be "slow to speak and swift to hear," so that we might hear those words of direction, "This is the way, walk in it."

QUOTE FOR TODAY: Religion drives men in the East to

lie on beds of nails, in the West to sit on hard pews . . . both are painful, to God and man.

* * *

FRIDAY

READING: Revelation 11:1-19

MEMORY VERSE: "Then the seventh angel sounded: And there were loud voices in heaven, saying, 'The kingdoms of this world have become the kingdoms of our Lord and of His Christ, and He shall reign forever and ever!'" Revelation 11:15

I am continually amazed at how many Bible "types" are hidden in the Scriptures. One, which I saw for the first time recently, is hidden in the pages of the book of Esther. In Chapter 3, we find that the King, whom I see as a Bible type of God, promoted Haman, typical of Lucifer before the fall. Verse 1 says that the King promoted Haman and "advanced him," and "set his seat above all the princes who were with him." Such was the case with Lucifer before he was cast down as lightning from his place of honor. The prince power of the air had a place of exaltation, described so vividly for us in Ezekiel Chapter 28.

The story continues in Esther, telling us of Mordecai (a type of Christ) and his refusal to bow down and pay homage to Haman. Haman's reaction was that he was "full of wrath." The same words are used to describe Lucifer or Satan. The Son of God refused to bow down and worship him, and now the Scriptures tell us satan is filled with wrath. Haman complained saying, "There is a certain people scattered abroad and dispersed among the people in all the provinces, and their laws are different from all people." Haman's wrath was manifest in a hatred for Mordecai's people, the Jews, and satan's hatred is not only toward Jesus, but  all who belong to Him. Notice Haman's words describing the Jews as being "scattered abroad and dispersed." Similar words are used to describe the people of God at the beginning of the Epistles.

We also have "laws which are different from all people" -- the "Law of Liberty" and the "Law of life in Christ Jesus." Further on in Chapter 3 of Esther we find that Haman sought to "kill and destroy" all Jews, both young and old. The same words are used of satan in John Chapter 10 -- he came to "kill, steal and destroy."

The story climaxes when Haman builds a gallows to hang Mordecai, but things turn sour on him and he is actually hung upon his own gallows. Praise God, in the same way, the very cross upon which satan sought to destroy the Son of God became the instrument of his defeat, and also the means of deliverance for every Christian who was once subject to his power.

QUOTE FOR TODAY: "The Christian world is in a dead

sleep. Nothing but a loud voice can awaken them out of it."
- George Whitefield

* * *

SATURDAY

READING: Psalm 32

MEMORY VERSE: "Blessed is he whose transgression is forgiven, whose sin is covered." Psalm 32:1

A friend and I were once walking through a Botanical Garden when a minister wearing a white collar walked by, followed by a group of very elderly, chattering ladies. My friend remarked that such a scene typified the world's view of the church. They don't see it as a glorious church with the very God of Glory in the midst, but as elderly men, drinking cups of tea with groups of chattering, knitting-needle-laden, elderly women.

The Christian has a different view of God, the Bible, prayer and the church. To him, God is the mighty Creator of all things, the One in whom dwells all power, authority and wisdom. He is the one who causes lightning to flash, thunder to roar, the sun to shine, who is the very sustainer and source of all life.

But to the average sinner, God is that old man who sits on a throne in the sky. He has a long flowing beard, and you pray to him when Grandma gets sick.

To the Christian, prayer is the very power-house of God. Prayer is the life-line by which mortal man may commune with the Creator of the universe.

Prayer is the mystery by which Almighty God calls upon man to "stand in the gap," to intercede on behalf of the very nations of this world. Prayer is the source of the Christian's strength, the very key with which he "unlocks every day and the bolt by which he closes the door of each night."

Yet, the world's view of prayer was summed up in the following incident. A non-Christian friend phoned me and said, "I telephoned before, but you were saying your prayers."

The impression I received was the thought that I was on my knees with my hands cupped, saying, "God bless Grandma and Grandpa, etc" . . . teddy bear close at hand.

Such a notion is the reproach we must bear, until God opens the eyes of those whom the "god of this world" has blinded.

The ungodly are truly like a man who has been born blind. The Bible tells us that the natural man cannot receive the things of the Spirit of God, they are without his ability.

His "understanding is darkened," and there is no way he can see until God gives him light, that he may know the truth; and that he might see "the light of the glorious Gospel of Christ who is the image of God."

QUOTE FOR TODAY: "Our absolute obedience to Him

is a manifestation of our absolute love for Him." - George
Otis, Jr.

* * *

SUNDAY

READING: Psalm 77:1-20

MEMORY VERSE: "Your way, O God, is in the sanctu-
ary; Who is so great a God as our God?" Psalm 77:13

Something I recently have found to be rather painful, is
the amount of publicity given to professing ministries of the
Gospel who deny the Scriptures and the fundamentals of the
Christian faith. By their own profession, these are uncon-
verted men masquerad-
ing as part of the Chris-
tian flock. They are of
the world, they speak as
the world, and the world
loves it and gives the
press as a pulpit to
preach their profanity.

Some time ago, I felt
so stirred that I placed a
reasonable-sized adver-
tisement in the newspa-
per, offering one thou-
sand dollars to anyone
who could prove to me there was even one mistake in the
Word of God. As usual, noone came forward to claim the

"easy cash." Quite frankly, I have been quite ready for battle, both barrels loaded, but it seems that the enemy's ammunition is nothing but bluff.

It would also seem from Scripture that this generation has even fewer "hedges" to hide behind than generations of the past. For example, previous generations could have pointed to the words of Jesus as being unfulfilled in Matthew 24 and Luke 21 where He spoke of the Jews obtaining Jerusalem. Not so since 1967, when Israel obtained Jerusalem for the first time in nearly 2,000 years fulfilling the words of the Son of God.

Generations of the past no doubt pointed to that obvious error in the book of Job where it clearly speaks of the earth "hanging upon nothing." Only recently has science dropped its foolish theories and agreed with the Bible when it speaks of earth's free float in space. Another "mistake" is the Bible's insistence that the earth is round. Everybody knew it was flat until Magellan's crew came back up around the other side. Three thousand years after the Bible stated that the moon doesn't shine with its own light, man invented the telescope and realized that the moon merely reflects the sun's rays.

My strongest reason for believing the Bible isn't necessarily the scientific facts contained within its pages, but the fact that I have met the author. When God's Spirit enters a person, his mind is enlightened, he is given spiritual understanding and thus can stand upon the promises of the Word with confidence, knowing that all Scripture is given by inspiration of God. How true are the words of Mark Twain, "It's not the things I cannot understand in the Bible that worry me but the things that I can understand."

QUOTE FOR TODAY: "No man is really consecrated until his money is dedicated." - Roy L. Smith

* * *

MONDAY

READING: Micah 6:1-16

MEMORY VERSE: "He has shown you, O man, what is good; and what does the Lord require of you, but to do justly, to love mercy, and to walk humbly with your God?" Micah 6:8

As an introduction to a sermon at a recent youth rally, I showed how I had a few days earlier spoken at a University on the subjects of homosexuality, abortion, the occult and

rock music. After the conclusion of the rally, a rather irate young lady came up to me and asked what right I had to stand up and condemn abortion. She looked a little taken back when I said, "I didn't condemn abortion; you just assumed I did." She then apologized and was about to leave when I asked her if she would like to know my views on the subject. I then said, "Abortion is murder. The life of the flesh is in the blood, none of us have the right to take the life of a child."

It turned out that this young lady, who was a professing Christian, had had an abortion and there was no way she was going to change her views. I showed her portions of Scripture which tell us that God knows of us as we are being formed in the womb.

We are not just a piece of mucus, but a living identity. She was not moved by the authority of Scripture, a photo of a dead, aborted child in a bucket, nor the testimony of medical science which spoke of the baby's heart beating 14-28 days after conception.

Sadly, her case was typical of many a "pro-abortionist." Rather than admit guilt and let the blood of Christ cleanse an evil conscience, the plea is, "I am innocent," followed by attempts to justify the action.

This is also the case with the homosexual who, rather than turn from his error, gives himself over to it: "Who, knowing the righteous judgment of God, that those who practice such things are worthy of death, not only do the same but also approve those who practice them." (Romans 1:32)

Unfortunately, if this young woman keeps condoning abortion, she will not only be guilty of murder in the sight of God, but she will encourage others to commit murder, thus adding to her sins.

Just as Adam tried to hide from God because of sin, so all of us, have at one time or another, attempted such folly. However, God's grace is there for all who will come and admit responsibility, and ask for cleansing and forgiveness.

QUOTE FOR TODAY: "Prayer reaches out in love to a

dying world and says, I care." - Dick Eastman

* * *

TUESDAY

READING: Psalm 86:1-17

MEMORY VERSE: "But You, O Lord, are a God full of compassion, and gracious, longsuffering and abundant in mercy and truth." Psalm 86:15

I was once in a plane which was just about to land at one of our major airports when I noticed the rather robust lady next to me had a look of terror in her eyes. I leaned over to her and said that if she was afraid she was welcome to hold my hand. In an instant she gripped my hand like a vice. I watched as my fingers turned white with her grip. I thought "Great, she's still in terror, and now I'm in pain."

I began thinking of this incident and praying about it as potential sermon material. I imagined what the outcome would have been, if I had turned to her and said, "You don't need to fear lady, I know the pilot personally. He is a man of tremendous ability. He's never even had a minor accident while flying. He could fly this plane with his hands tied behind his back. Couple this with the fact that he has spent years in training with the most up to date equipment and you will realize that your fears are totally unfounded."

If that had been the case, I would have been releasing that woman from fear by building a respect for the pilot by speaking of his amazing ability; then it was up to her to receive that knowledge and act upon it accordingly. If she believed me she may have said, "Is that so, really? Is he that good . . . I feel much better now." She had chosen to have faith and thus been released from fear. In the same way, as we gain knowledge of God through the Word, we gain a respect or reverence for Him. We see our Pilot, the Captain of our salvation, as having tremendous ability, and therefore choose faith even on the bumpiest flight.

I was meditating on these thoughts while flying recently. The stewardess announced that we were about to hit turbulence and in her words, "but the captain is going to try and get her down." As we circled the airport the captain announced, "I just missed the runway, but I'll try again." He did, and we landed in blustery conditions with one wheel on the runway, but the other still 2-3 feet off the ground, much to my horror.

Three days later I was flying home, when I joined the pilots on the flight deck. One was a Christian so he invited me to stay up front for the landing. I remarked on the perfect landing to which he replied, in jest (I hope), "We just close our eyes for the last five feet!"

Four days later, Sue and I were waiting to go on another flight. We assured ourselves of the ability of these pilots, and faith arose. As we were awaiting takeoff the captain announced, "Welcome to flight 266." Sue remarked that it was actually flight 226. Then the captain said conditions at our destination were, "Gustily westy winds." I cringed as I hoped that his ability to fly was better than his reading and speaking. Sadly, it was too late for me to get off. I am still not really sure if God had a purpose in allowing such incidents to come my way, but I am inclined to think that perhaps He is showing me that He does have a sense of humor.

QUOTE FOR TODAY: "The way of this world is to praise dead saints and persecute living ones." - Nathaniel Howe

* * *

WEDNESDAY

READING: Psalm 78:1-20

MEMORY VERSE: "We will not hide them from their children, telling the generation to come the praises of the Lord, and His strength and His wonderful works that He has done." Psalm 78:4

A number of years ago, I laid down on the white sands of one of the most beautiful beach resorts in the world. I could feel the warmth of the sunlight as I listened to the waves gently lap the shore. As I lay there, I thought, *"How utterly boring!"*

I remember laughing to myself that I should have such a thought. Millions would give their right arm to "get away from it all." It's the dream of multitudes to be free from the dull routine of daily drudgery and find such a beach resort. But I can say "it's boring" and still laugh about it. I can imagine the horror coming over the elite as they buy their own island or beach and sit back to take their ease, and yet come to the same revelation. Perhaps some, who are less

fortunate mentally, may be able to lay week after week, month after month, year after year; but the average person, given such a lifestyle is almost driven "around the bend."

As a child, I remember seeing a television program which showed millionaires who were making such a phenomenal amount of money that it couldn't be calculated. Some of these people took their homemade lunch to work even though they could afford to buy paradise islands and spend their lives basking on sun-baked beaches. They chose to do the "9:00 - 5:00 thing."

Why is it that those who dream of such a lifestyle are those who could never attain it, and those who attain the means wouldn't dream of it? -- they prefer the daily drudge. The answer is in the book of Romans Chapter 8: "For the creation was subjected to futility, not willingly, but because of Him who subjected it in hope." In other words God has subjected humanity to futility. Those who seek for "worldly pleasure," (for want of a better word) are usually those who have never attained it for any length of time, and thus have never experienced its futility. Solomon, with all his wealth and pleasure, cried in despair, "Vanity, vanity, all is vanity." But I can laugh when I'm bored with the world's so called pleasures, because I have been set free from "the bondage of corruption into the glorious liberty of the children of God." By the power of the Spirit of the living God, I have had a foretaste of the world to come, and believe me, we "who have the first fruits of the Spirit, even we ourselves groan within ourselves, waiting for the adoption, that is the redemption of our body."

QUOTE FOR TODAY: "All Christians are obligated to work as if they do not believe in prayer and pray as if they do not believe in work." - Leonard Ravenhill

* * *

THURSDAY

READING: Psalm 105:1-22

MEMORY VERSE: "Oh, give thanks to the Lord! Call upon His name; make known His deeds among the peoples." Psalm 105:1

C.S. Lewis spoke of two dangers of the demonic realm. One was to have an unhealthy pre-occupation with them, and the other was to not believe in them at all. Scripture seems to take it for granted that the Christian is aware of the enemy with the words, "for we are not ignorant of his devices," and I trust that common sense will guard us from the extreme.

A very valuable lesson was learned, I'm sure, by a number of young people at a recent youth rally. Just before I was due to speak, a group of youths embarked upon a drama in which they demonstrated evil with "heavy metal" rock music. The crowd was hushed as the lights were dimmed. One could certainly say that the music created the desired atmosphere of evil. Suddenly, in the midst of the crowd a young man manifested demons. He screamed and fell on the floor as the spirit "rent him sore." Someone yelled for the lights to be put on. Slowly the congregation began to sing "There's Power in the Blood." The young man was led outside, the drama abandoned, the confusion lifted, and I very quickly changed my message to rock music and the occult. Although I'm sure many found that incident frightening, I must say that it was one way to have my message received with sobriety. When I spoke of the power of heavy metal occultic-based rock music everyone knew what I meant.

After the meeting, as I began to reflect on the incident, I thought of the portion of Scripture in 2 Corinthians 6:14 " . . . for what fellowship has righteousness with lawlessness? And what communion has light with darkness?" That incident was a clear demonstration that God is holy. He is "light and in him is no darkness at all." We had asked God to be present in our midst yet had attempted to use that which is abominable to minister to the ungodly. David Bowie was right when he said, "Rock and roll is the devil's music." It would seem he is convinced, while multitudes of naive Christians are not.

Let's all learn a lesson from such folly and take heed to the following Scripture, without any Pharisaic, monasterial attitude: "And what accord has Christ with Belial? Or what part has a believer with an unbeliever? And what agreement has the temple of God with idols? For you are the temple of the living God. As God has said: I will dwell in them and walk among them. I will be their God and they shall be My people. Therefore come out from among them and be separate, says the Lord. Do not touch what is unclean, and I will receive you. I will be a Father to you, and you shall be My sons and daughters, says the Lord Almighty."

QUOTE FOR TODAY: "You are either a missionary or a mission field: one of the two." - Olaf Skinsnes

* * *

FRIDAY

READING: Proverbs 4:1-27

MEMORY VERSE: "Ponder the path of your feet, and let all your ways be established." Proverbs 4:26

Most of us realize that a child learns much during the "four to ten year old" bracket. His knowledge moves from almost zero to a fantastic accumulation in a relatively short period of time. His mind is filled with questions, and that is precisely what causes him to grow.

The same thing applies spiritually. The new Christian is filled with questions about the Kingdom of God. The more questions, the quicker the growth. God forbid that the time would come when each of us reaches that point of thinking that we "know it all." Questions are a healthy sign. We should, even as mature Christians, approach each portion of Scripture with a, "Why is that?" Not as the ungodly, in a rebellious unbelief, but in sincerity, seeking to uncover the gems of truth hidden from the so-called "wise and prudent."

Such was the case recently when my wife and I were reading the Word together. We were reading the parable of the five foolish and the five wise virgins. I remarked to Sue that I could understand the meaning of the parable right up until the point where the foolish virgins ran out of oil. The part  which left me in the dark was where the wise virgins, said to the foolish, ". . . but go rather to those who sell, and buy for yourselves." My interpretation (which is open to correction) is that the wise virgins are genuine converts, the foolish are "false brethren." The lamps are typical of the Word of God (Psalm 119:105), and the oil, of the Holy Spirit; but why did the wise virgins say that it could be bought. Salvation is by grace, through faith. It cannot be earned or even deserved. Praise God -- He heard my question and gave me the answer the very next morning. Often we think that to buy we need to exchange money, but this is not so with salvation. Look at the words of Isaiah in his universal call to salvation, "Ho! Everyone who thirsts, come to the waters; and you who have no money, come, buy and eat. Yes, come, buy wine and milk without money and without price" (Isaiah 55:1). Salvation comes through purchase, but not a purchase using money, because it is "without price."

The means of exchange is to give Him your life. He doesn't want yours, but you. Through such an exchange you only give that which you could not keep, and gain that which you cannot lose.

QUOTE FOR TODAY: "Be united with other Christians. A wall with loose bricks is not good. The bricks must be cemented together." - Corrie Ten Boom

* * *

SATURDAY

READING: Proverbs 12:1-28

MEMORY VERSE: "In the way of righteousness is life, and in its pathway there is no death." Proverbs 12:28

The Bible tells us that the steps of a good man are ordered by the Lord. If you are trusting in Jesus Christ as Savior and serving Him as Lord, you can claim that very promise. No matter where you go in life, you can trust that your steps are being "ordered by the Lord." No matter what happens to you, you can have a confident assurance that the hand of Almighty God is guiding and directing your paths.

Such was the case recently when we had a minor problem with the return spring on the accelerator of our car. We pulled into the local shop and a serviceman in his late thirties began to look at the problem. I began to make small talk by asking if he enjoyed his work, and was a little taken back by his reply. He said, "I hate it . . . I would rob banks if I didn't get caught." I found such a statement tre-

mendously thought-provoking. I wonder how many people would turn to crime if they knew that they never would be punished. Crime is already a source of income for millions, despite the threat of recompense.

Some time later, our disgruntled mechanic friend returned with a spring in hand but with-

out one in his step. As he worked over the motor I began to share with him the cause of his restlessness. He had no peace in his heart, thus whatever he put his hand to he would find futile, until he found peace with God. I told him that he needed to become a "Christian." His reply was a frank, "Been there, done that." It turned out that he had been a Methodist until he was 16 years old. They couldn't answer his questions, so he dropped it.

Sadly, my friend had "thrown out the baby with the bath water." He had now put his efforts into Buddhism, something very evident by his lack of joy. He was another one who had studied the meal, so to speak, but had failed to taste. No wonder he left hungry. Only those who actually obey the command of Jesus to be born again can know the truth of the words, "O taste and see that the Lord is good."

QUOTE FOR TODAY: "It is not our comment on the Word that saves, but the Word itself." - Robert Murray McCheyne

* * *

SUNDAY

READING: Psalm 89:1-29

MEMORY VERSE: "For who in the heavens can be compared to the Lord." Psalm 89:6a

The gang problem in L.A. is out of control. Every weekend, without fail, there are multiple gang killings. It's not unusual to have seven or eight members killed on one weekend, a mother shot, or a child killed in a driveby shooting. One even hears tragic stories of people being shot and killed just because they are wearing the wrong color clothing. The gangs are known by their different colors. If an innocent party finds himself wearing a blue shirt in a red area, that can be to his death. One man found himself lost one day while driving and ended up in a dead end street. He was shot to death because he was wearing the wrong colors.

When Ken, a muscular Sheriff-Lieutenant who went to our church, asked if I would be interested in looking through the L.A. County Jail, I jumped at the chance. As the jail was in downtown L.A., I decided to call in at Fifth Street and feed the homeless on the way. Ken had previously  asked if he could join us on outreach, so it was a chance to kill two birds with one stone. Two other friends, Mike and another Ken, the church administrator, decided they would also like to tour the jail.

Within two minutes of parking in Fifth Street, a crowd of about one hundred, mainly men, lined up for food. The last time I spoke they seemed very restless, so I decided to try something a little different this time. I often use "sleight-of-hand" to get people's attention but I'd never used it on Fifth Street before. The trick is very simple and extremely effective. I take a scarf in my right hand, put it into my left hand and make it disappear. Then I make it appear again before speaking on the fact that the eyes aren't trustworthy. It worked. For the first time in weeks, I had their attention. They were actually looking my way and even listening to what I said. I could hear them saying, "How'd you do dat?" -- *"Do dat again!"* So I did. I took the red scarf from my right hand and put it into my left." Then I spoke, we gave out food, and then got into the van.

As Ken sat his brawny body in the passenger seat, he looked at me with a rather sober look and said, "Next time you do that trick, use a green scarf!" Suddenly, it dawned on me what I had just done. When I was doing the trick, he could hear voices saying, *"This is a blue neighborhood!"* and "That's a *red* scarf!" I hadn't merely worn a red shirt in a blue area . . . I had waved a red scarf in their face! My guardian angel must be gray! Tomorrow, I will share with you about our tour through the L.A. County Jail.

QUOTE FOR TODAY: "Life begins when you get out of the grandstand, into the game." - P.L. DeBevoise

* * *

MONDAY

READING: Psalm 89:30-52

MEMORY VERSE: "What man can live and not see death? Can he deliver his life from the power of the grave?" Psalm 89:48

Yesterday, we looked at how a friend invited me to the Los Angeles County Jail. After we fed the homeless, Ken said he had a different attitude than most as we gave out the food. He didn't mind the fact that many were so deceitful and sneaked around to the back of the line for more and that they would take food for themselves and let others go hungry. After twenty years in the police force he knew that each one of those men who took food from us would stab you in the back as quick as look at you. Although I didn't like to think too much about it, he was right.

Twenty-three thousand are housed in the jail-system of L.A. Six thousand were in the building in which Ken worked. After surrendering our driver's license for I.D. we began our tour. It is an awesome thing to see human beings who are in debt

to the law. There were cells for suicidal inmates, crazy inmates, murderers and those going through drug withdrawal. We walked in front of men who had become trophies of Hell -- men who mumbled nonsensical words at us as we walked by their cage. One grabbed the bars of his eight by five foot cell and screamed in torment that he needed help for his mental condition. I felt overwhelmed with pity then anger as, without a break, he went right into a speel about how he hated blacks. Then he shifted gear into saluting the officers that were showing us around.

Nowadays, as customers are welcomed into the jail-system, authorities have a complete background on where they are from, and past criminal records. Big problems will develop if different gangs are mixed in together. But, thanks to the push of a computer keyboard, the gangs can be put in with their "own groups."

We were shown the death row cells and even a series of windowless rooms in which special prisoners were kept. When we came out, one of the officers said that very few people were allowed in there. I asked why we were allowed in, to which he said, "Well you're not going to give them anything!" I don't think he saw the prisoner reading a tract.

It was only after an hour or so of hearing everyone calling Ken, "Sir," that I found out he was the boss of this area. His job was to prepare the thousand new customers brought in to the prison system each day. I felt as though I was looking back into the seventeenth century as I peered at about a hundred fifty men chained to each other. They were then unchained and herded into a room where they were categorized and strip searched. More than once, as I passed groups of prisoners, I would say, "Hiya guys" and get a warm response from some. Others would stare back with the warmth of dry ice. Thank God there are Christian officers in that prison who are praying for those men. L.A. County Jail is such a cold, hard place; yet it is warm and soft compared to some prisons in other countries. How horrible to be in debt to man's law. How fearful to be in debt to the Law of a holy God.

QUOTE FOR TODAY: Sin's misery and God's mercy are beyond measure.

* * *

TUESDAY

READING: Proverbs 19:1-29

MEMORY VERSE: "A false witness will not go unpunished, and he who speaks lies will not escape." Proverbs 19:5

I find the most difficult thing about witnessing is bringing up the subject of God. There is always a fear of rejection I have to overcome. Well, how would you like to meet a stranger, build a bond with him, then within *two minutes* know his intimate beliefs about God, sin, Judgment Day and where he stands regarding his salvation -- all without any offense. You can, by using our IQ cards. Sue and I are the directors of Living Waters Publications, a non-profit ministry which has printed millions of tracts.

One of our tracts is called, *"Natural Enquiry News,"* and is printed on a one page format similar to a well-known tabloid. The headlines include, "Man cuts up raped wife," "Woman's body savaged by vicious dogs!" "Fat man found murdered on bathroom floor!" On the reverse side it reveals that each  of these brutal incidents are found in the Bible, saying that God doesn't hide men's sins but exposes them, warning that He will one day judge the world in righteousness. People can't resist them.

When I approach a group of young people, I just say, "Wanna read something violent?" and as they start taking them I say, " . . . it's really sick!" They go like hot cakes. My favorite tract is the IQ Test. This small card has two tests. After personally giving out an estimated 50,000 - 60,000 tracts, I have found the following principles most successful: 1/ Keep the cards in your wallet. 2/ As you approach a stranger, get one out of the wallet while saying, "Did you get one of these?" This has a three-fold effect. First, the person knows you are giving him something of value because it comes out of your wallet. Second, the question has the effect of stimulating curiosity. And third, it makes him feel he is missing out on something (which he is, if he doesn't take it).

Most at this point will ask, "One of what?" When you answer "It's an IQ Test," they usually smile -- which is very strange, but pleasant when giving out a Christian tract. They even do the simple test right away. Nine out of ten fail and are amazed when you show them *where* they failed. Then they do Side 2, which is the Christian IQ test. This asks six very basic questions about God, sin, and salvation. The amazing thing is that after doing Side 1, the person usually obeys the instructions and reads Side 2 OUT LOUD, revealing to you exactly where he stands regarding the things of God. I have had many opportunities to witness, such as the time where a man did the test on Side 2. I checked his answers and said, "You did well -- four out of six. The two you missed were: "You said God's standards were the same as ours . . . when the Bible says they are not. His way is perfect. God requires us to be perfect in thought, word and deed. And you said you avoid Hell by living a "good" life, when the Bible says, 'not by works of righteousness has He saved us, but according to his mercy.' I was then able to go on and share the way of salvation through the Savior. The card does all the hard work -- it bridges the gap with strangers, inoffensively brings up the subject of the things of God, shows you where they stand spiritually, and gives you incredible openings to witness of your faith . . . *all in two minutes!* (I.Q. Cards are available through Living Waters Publications -- see the back pages of this book).

QUOTE FOR TODAY: Homework is what gives a youngster something to do while watching television.

* * *

WEDNESDAY

READING: Proverbs 20:1-30

MEMORY VERSE: "The glory of young men is their strength, and the splendor of old men is their gray head." Proverbs 20:29

I am sure you have young people within your church who are interested in drama. It does have its place within evangelism . . . as long as those who are involved remember that God has "chosen the foolishness of preaching to save them that believe" (1 Corinthians 1:21). It's not enough to leave the world entertained -- it needs to hear the Gospel expounded in truth. A drama should not only have some sort of message, it should also get a crowd for the preacher to share the Word, which is able to save them from the wrath which is to come.

I got the idea for the following drama while on a plane, from part of the prelude to a movie. Imagine if you will, a crowded beach or park. Suddenly, a boom box begins to play loud music with a very heavy beat. A dozen or so people begin doing aerobics. Each is dressed in aerobic gear, and work out with the utmost enthusiasm. They are being led by a joy-filled, life-loving, sweat-band-clad instructor.

The team duplicates his every move with the utmost fervor, yelling with unadulterated joy and excitement. They love every minute. A crowd gathers to watch. About half way through the fitness-filled aerobics routine, the instructor suddenly pulls a facial expression of extreme pain and thumps his  chest with both fists, obviously having a heart attack. The team duplicates this "new move," each pounding his own chest. The instructor staggers to the left. Watching his creative moves, the team, with simplistic diligence, also staggers to the left. He reels to the right; they copy each staggered step. Finally, with great drama, he collapses on his back . . . and with candid facial expressions and tireless enthusiasm, so does the team.

As they lie motionless on the ground someone steps forward and says, "Do you know that many people actually die healthy; that you are going to die whether you love life or hate it; whether you are fat or fit? -- all of us will eventually pass into death. We are all part of the ultimate statistic, "ten out of ten die." There is only one answer to man's greatest dilemma . . . and I want you to stay, just for a few minutes, and allow me to share it with you. The reason we die is because we have sinned against God; we have broken his Law . . . " etc.

One of the advantages of this drama is that it is so simple to do. It can't help but draw a crowd and will enable the preacher to hit listeners with the truth while they are still laughing . . . a very effective communication key.

QUOTE FOR TODAY: Life is a lot like tennis -- the one who serves the best seldom loses.

* * *

THURSDAY

READING: Hebrews 1:1-14

MEMORY VERSE: "But to the Son He says: 'Your throne, O God, is forever and ever; a scepter of righteousness is the scepter of Your Kingdom.'" Hebrews 1:8

An all time record for the longest lip-locking is held by a Mr. Peter Rowlands. When Mr. Rowlands found himself in conditions so freezing that he couldn't get his key into the lock of his car, he decided to use some ingenuity by blowing hot air into the lock. Unfortunately, his

warm lips touched the freezing metal and locked to it.

As he held fast with his lips on the lock and knees on the ground, an elderly woman stopped and enquired as to whether or not he was O.K. Mr. Rowlands replied, "Alra? Igmmlptk!!!" *at which the woman ran away.* He was actually trapped in that posture for twenty minutes until constant hot breathing brought him his freedom.

Speaking of lips, it seems obvious that God gave them to us for a number of reasons. They are ideal for the famished soul to lick before a mouth-watering meal. They are very flexible, stretching from a yawn, then contracting to accommodate the crinkle of a whistle. In fact, distasteful as it may seem, the pliant material used for the lips looks similar to that used in the manufacture of worms.

Lips are also items to read in pre-electoral presidential promises. However, I think that one of the best things that lips are made for, is kissing. Believe it or not, God did make lips to kiss and be kissed; the kiss being referred to approximately forty-five times in the Bible.

Those who put xxxx on the bottom of letters and cards to signify kisses, usually aren't aware that the custom goes back to the early Christian era. In those days the symbol was used to signify the cross of Calvary. When a document was signed, as many couldn't write, the symbol was used as a legally valid mark, and was often kissed by the signatory as a sign of sincerity. The practice of kissing the mark led to it becoming a symbol of a kiss.

During World War Two, British and American forces were forbidden from using the symbol on their letters, for fear of it being used to transmit coded messages.

Although it is possible to speak without moving your lips, it pays to use them if you want to be understood. May you and I always use our lips as vehicles for God's message to humanity, as well as offering "the sacrifice of praise to God, that is, the fruit of our lips, giving thanks to His name."

QUOTE FOR TODAY: When you know you have humility, you've lost it.

* * *

FRIDAY

READING: Hebrews 13:1-24

MEMORY VERSE: "Pray for us; for we are confident that we have a good conscience, in all things desiring to live honorably." Hebrews 13:18

In July of 1988, a 49 year old rancher in Idaho was dismounting his still running tractor when he stood on a gob of grease. As he slipped, he grabbed the control bar for support. This put the tractor in gear. It lunged forward and he was thrown off balance, hitting the throttle lever. He then fell to the ground in front of the wheel of the now moving tractor.

Unfortunately, he had filled the 18" wide tires with water to give it more traction. It worked. As the 9600 pound tractor ran over his body he felt his pelvic bones breaking. The tractor then drove over his chest breaking ribs as it did so, and just missing his head.

As the farmer lay in the dirt, his only consoling thought was the fact that the tractor would hit the fence and alert his

neighbors that something was wrong. Not so. It hit a hay bale, jerking the front wheels to one side, did a complete circle around the field and came for him a second time. As it headed for him, he mustered all his energy and rolled his shattered body out of its path. Safe! Nope. It hit an oil can, turning its front wheels to one side *and it came around the field again!* This time it ran over his legs! The poor man was found some time later, and lived to face a $40,000 medical bill.

Now, here's a very sobering thought. *That man may have been a Christian.* If that's so, it is difficult to reconcile how God could allow so many horrible circumstances to come to one of His children. Yet, I know of many cases where unspeakable suffering and storms of everyday living have hit both the Christian as well as the non-Christian.

Someone once said we need to go and minister to the gangs of L.A. Then he said, "God will protect us from the bullets." I think that the statement needs qualification. I am not saying that God won't divinely intervene if someone wants to kill me, but I'm saying it is not always the case. Take for instance the case of Stephen. He was stoned to death for the cause of the Gospel. God in His great wisdom didn't intervene. James was beheaded for the Gospel, and once again God didn't intervene. John the Baptist was also beheaded, and tradition tells us that all the disciples except

John were murdered for the cause of the Gospel. If you read *Foxes Book of Martyrs,* you will see that literally millions have died for Christ. When the Bible promises "not a hair on your head shall perish," it can either mean that we will be saved from God's wrath on the Day of Judgment or that death will deliver us from this life into Heaven. While God did protect and deliver Paul many times, tradition tells us that he did end up being martyred.

Don't be disillusioned if you are hated for His name's sake, or physically persecuted as a Christian, or a tractor runs over your legs; it doesn't mean God has forsaken you. He will never forsake His own. Remember that God is in control, that nothing happens without His permission, but don't presume that you will escape persecution if you live godly in Christ Jesus. Just keep your eyes on the cross; that's proof of God's love for you, and thank Him that the sufferings of this world are not worthy to be compared to the glory that shall be ours.

QUOTE FOR TODAY: Better to be patient on the road, than a patient in the hospital.

* * *

SATURDAY

READING: Genesis 2:1-25

MEMORY VERSE: "And the Lord God formed man of the dust of the ground, and breathed into his nostrils the breath of life; and the man became a living soul." Genesis 2:7

Those of us who have experienced the power of Jesus Christ know what the Bible means when it says, "If any man be in Christ, he is a new creature; old things pass away, behold, all things become new." I am still in a state of shock after many years since my conversion. A young Christian,

not really knowing what he was doing, brought me to a knowledge of salvation over a six hour period. A car filled with surfers left for a surfing trip speaking of things young men often do; three days later, back we came, singing hymns! We *were* new creatures.

Another memorable incident happened that same weekend. I had been using a spray-on deodorant for three or four days. The day after my conversion, when I went to put on the deodorant, I noticed that the label said, "Spray into the air for three or four seconds;" *I had been using air freshener!* The incident came to mind recently after I purchased some eye drops for itching eyes.

One morning, I asked my daughter to put the drops into my eyes. I had already taken the drops from the cupboard, so I gave her the bottle and she did the deed. That evening I asked my wife if she would be kind enough to drop a few drips in. As she did so, Rachel, my daughter said, *"That wasn't what I put in this morning!"* I had handed her drops for nasal congestion! Some things never change. My problem, once again, was that I hadn't bothered to read the instructions.

This same problem is so prevalent in the world, particularly in the area of marriage. So few bother to see what the Bible, God's Instruction Book, has to say on the subject. God, the creator of marriage, gives clear instructions in His Word on how to make a marriage work. It speaks of wives honoring and submitting to husbands, and husbands loving their wives "as Christ loved the Church and gave Himself for it." Many a woman's libber breaks out in goosebumps at the very thought of submission. They can't see the honorable place of love and esteem women are given by having their husbands love them as Christ loved the Church. What woman doesn't want to be honored and loved? When the Bible speaks of submission, it does not mean that the wife is to walk four paces behind her whip-lashing master. The problem is, so few in the world get to see how good it is to have a marriage in the order that God has given. Those who esteem God's Word within their home, don't live for themselves but first and foremost for God. That's what the Book says, and what's more, it works.

QUOTE FOR TODAY: "Right is right, even if everyone is against it; and wrong is wrong, even if everyone is for it." - William Penny

* * *

SUNDAY

READING: 1 Kings 11:1-43

MEMORY VERSE: "For it came to pass, when Solomon was old, that his wives turned away his heart after other gods: and his heart was not perfect with the Lord his God, as was the heart of David his father." 1 Kings 11:4

If there is one thing I don't normally get bothered with its headaches. However, on one particular day I was preparing a word on the occult when suddenly a migraine headache came upon me. I hadn't had a migraine like that since I went for a surf in my teens on a very frosty day. As I kept writing, the headache grew worse. The main symptom was an impairment of sight.

After about half an hour in this condition, I noticed a woman had entered our store (which we had at the time); she was having trouble breathing. After serving her I asked if I could pray for her condition. As I stood there talking to her I could hardly see because of the migraine. I prayed that God would completely heal her of her bronchial condition. I don't know the outcome of the prayer for the woman, but one thing I do know, is that when I opened my eyes I was the one who had been healed!! Praise God, my sight was restored completely!

The Bible gives us a wonderful principle in the closing chapter of the book of Job -- "And the Lord turned the captivity of Job, when he prayed for his friends." This same principle is also related in John Chapter 13:

"So after he had washed their feet, and had taken his garments, and was set down again, he said unto them, know you what I have done for you? You call me Master and Lord: and you say well; for so I am. If I then, your Lord and Master, have washed your feet; you also ought to wash one another's feet.

For I have given you an example, that you should do as I have done to you. Verily, verily, I say unto you. The servant is not greater than his lord; neither he that is sent greater than he that sent him. If ye know these things, happy are ye if ye do them."

What Jesus was saying is that if you will take upon yourself the humble attitude of "foot-washing" your brethren (which doesn't necessarily mean the physical act), this will be a tremendous source of happiness to you. I know a number of people whom I would term "joyless Christians."

As one probes into their attitude one finds a common denominator of selfishness. They are not happy because the only feet they wash are their own. They don't bother with anyone else but themselves.

The way to be released from such a miserable existence is to put into practice the words of Jesus -- Give yourself away in service to others.

There are many practical ways in which you can help others. Perhaps you could call your pastor and ask if there is anyone in the church who needs help or who just needs a visit. Take some flowers to an elderly person, visit a hospital or nursing home. Instead of saying, "I could never do that" say, "I can do all things through Christ who strengthens me" and that includes approaching a stranger in a hospital or home and saying, "You don't know me but I just came by to see if you are in need of anything." Show an interest in him, and watch for the look in his eyes as he begins to realize that someone really does care for him. Then, watch the change in your own life as you begin to experience the truth of the words, "If you know these things, happy are you if you do them."

QUOTE FOR TODAY: "The best way to revive a church is to build a fire in the pulpit." - D.L. Moody

* * *

MONDAY

READING: 2 Kings 5:1-27

MEMORY VERSE: "So he went down and dipped seven times in the Jordan, according to the saying of the man of God; and his flesh was restored like the flesh of a little child, and he was clean." 2 Kings 5:14

I'm sure you have had the experience of smelling something or hearing a song that sparks off a memory from the distant past. This happened to me as I was gazing into the bottom of a near empty honey jar. Suddenly, memories from my childhood lizard-catching days sprang to mind.

I would (with great skill and humility) catch lizards, then feed them honey off the end of a match stick. The smell of the honey brought back the memory. I regularly have the memory floodgates opened to my childhood years when I hear a song by the Beatles. Sometimes the memories can be pleasant, sometimes unpleasant.

Such incidents remind us that locked up within the corridors of our memory banks are experiences of the past. What we do today, will be a locked in the memory of tomorrow.

Some time ago, I sat next to a man in a plane on its way to another city. As I began chatting with this man in his mid-thirties, I found that he was an undertaker, or as he termed it, "funeral director." We had a very interesting conversation and I was able to share with him the fact that one day, in the not too distant future, his thriving industry was going to be out of work. Jesus Christ, the undertaker's nightmare, will completely destroy death and glorify the bodies of those who trust in Him!

One thing my new found friend related to me was the fact that so many of his customers (family and friends of the deceased) were riddled with guilt. They were almost driven insane because they had wronged the person who had died, and they had no means of seeking an avenue of forgiveness. Society is full of people who live in a perpetual state of remorse.

Perhaps you have wronged someone, yet at the present moment in time, seeking their forgiveness is not on your priority list. Perhaps your pride is holding you back from them, but know for sure, that one day, this day will only be a memory. It will be the day you had opportunity to ask them to forgive you. The memory of this day will either be pleasant or it will be bitter, depending on what you do with it. If your conscience is speaking to you right now, obey it. Perhaps the person will laugh at you, perhaps there will be reconciliation. Whatever happens, the point is, you will be doing what you know you should, and your memories will be a source of joy, rather than a source of remorse.

QUOTE FOR TODAY: "The one concern of the devil is to keep Christians from praying. He fears nothing from prayerless studies, prayerless work, and prayerless religion. He laughs at our toil, mocks at our wisdom, but trembles when we pray." - Samuel Chadwick

* * *

TUESDAY

READING: Psalms 1 & 2

MEMORY VERSE: "The Lord knows the way of the righteous, but the way of the ungodly shall perish." Psalm 1:6

The next few days of *Words of Comfort* are going to be a little different from the normal daily reading. I want to take you through the Ten Commandments. My reason for doing this is two-fold. First, and this may sound a little strange, I want to make sure you are truly saved. Many people go to church, read their Bibles, pray and are even committed enough to go through a devotional book such as this, and still are strangers to salvation. The reason for this is plain. They have never been told what sin is. They were told that they wouldn't find what they were looking for until they gave their hearts to Jesus. Nowhere in Scripture are we told to "give our hearts to Jesus." We are told to repent and place our faith in Jesus Christ. This is something we cannot do if we don't know what sin is. Sin is transgression of the Law (1 John 3:4). Paul said that he didn't know what sin was without the Law (Romans 7:7). So that you might make your "calling and election sure," we will take the time to open up the commandments.

The second reason for going through the Law is to equip those of you who are totally sure of your salvation. You need to take the time to get familiar with each Commandment to a point where you can, by memory, not only recall each, but also open it up and share with the unsaved what they mean in the light of New Testament revelation.

As we do go through the Law, remember these three facts: 1/ God sees the sins of your youth, as though it were yesterday. Just as time doesn't forgive transgression of civil law (i.e. a murderer is still a murderer twenty years after the crime), so time doesn't forgive sin. 2/ God sees your thought-life. He made the mind of man, so surely He can see what He made -- nothing is hidden from His omniscient eye. And 3/ He is perfect, just, good, holy and utterly righteous. By that, I mean by His very nature, He *must* punish transgression. If He sees a murder take place He must eventually bring the murderer to justice, something that the most dense of us can understand, even if there is disagreement on the *form* of punishment.

It is important to realize that being a Christian doesn't determine that you will live eternally; it just defines the *location*. If you die, as Jesus said, "in your sins," God will judge you accordingly. There is no place in Scripture for "purgatory" for a second chance.

The Bible reveals that you and I have failed to put God first, to love Him with heart, mind, soul and strength. It states plainly, "There is none that seeks after God; there is none that understands . . . " The First Commandment is to put God first in our affections. That's not an option, it's a command.

Tomorrow, we will look in depth at what the First of the Ten Commandments actually requires of humanity.

QUOTE FOR TODAY: You can give without loving, but you can't love without giving.

* * *

WEDNESDAY

READING: Psalms 3 & 4

MEMORY VERSE: "But you, O Lord, are a shield for me, my glory and the One who lifts up my head." Psalm 3:3

Imagine buying a child a toy for his pleasure, and having him love the toy more than he loved you. Yet, isn't that what you've done with God? Didn't He shower the gift of life upon you, giving you freedom, food, family, eyes, ears, a mind to think with? And you used that mind to deny the existence of the One who gave you the mind in the first place! Isn't it true that you have been guilty of complete and utter ingratitude.? If someone gave you a car as gift, should you thank him? Have you ever humbly thanked Him for the gift of life? If you have, but you've never obeyed His command to repent, then your "thanks" is nothing but empty hypocrisy.

If you love anything more than you love God, whether it is husband, wife, brother, sister, boyfriend, girlfriend, car, sport, or even your own life, you are loving the gift more than the Giver. What have you got that you didn't receive? Everything you have came to you via the goodness of

God. Jesus said that we should so love God that all our other affections for mother, father, brother, and sister, should seem as "hate" compared to the love we have for the God who gave them to us. It has been so rightly said that if the greatest commandment is to love God with all our heart, mind, soul and strength, then the greatest sin is failure to do so.

But more than that. The Bible says that the First Commandment also involves loving your neighbor as yourself. In the story Jesus gave of the Good Samaritan, the man picked up a beaten stranger, bathed his wounds, carried him to an inn, gave money for his care and said to the inn keeper that if he spent any more money while he was gone he would pay his expenses.

That is a picture of how God *commands* we should treat our fellow human beings. We should love them as much as we love ourselves . . . whether they be friend or foe. In fact, Jesus didn't call that story the "good" Samaritan; he wasn't "good," he merely carried out the basic requirements of the Law.

Have you loved humanity as yourself? You be the judge; have you kept the Law? Will you be innocent or guilty on Judgment Day? I'm not judging you -- I'm asking you to judge yourself. Sentence for transgression of the First Commandment is death.

Tomorrow, we will continue to look closely at the Ten Commandments.

QUOTE FOR TODAY: Think what others ought to be like, then start being that yourself.

* * *

THURSDAY

READING: Psalms 5 & 6

MEMORY VERSE: "Give ear to my words, O Lord, consider my meditation." Psalm 5:1

The Second Commandment is, "You shall not make yourself a graven image." (You won't find this in the Roman Catholic Bible; it was taken out because it exposed idolatry within the church. What they did was break the

Tenth Commandment up into two, to make up for the one they deleted). This command means that we shouldn't make a god in our own image, either with our hands or with our minds. I was guilty of this. I made a god to suit myself. My god didn't mind lust, a lie here or there; in fact he didn't have *any* moral dictates. But in truth, my god didn't exist. He was a figment of my imag . . . ination, shaped to conform to my sins. Almost all non-Christians have an idolatrous understanding of the nature of God.

Let me show you what I mean. Although the Bible says that humanity hates God without cause, most would deny that they do. You may not hate *your* god, but look at the Biblical revelation of our Creator. God killed a man in Genesis 38 because He didn't like his sexual activities. He commanded Joshua to kill every Canaanite man, woman and child, without mercy. He drowned the whole human race, but for eight people in the Noahic flood. He killed a man because he touched the Ark of the Covenant. He killed a husband and wife in the New Testament because they told one lie! Now, *that* God, says humanity, is not so easy to snuggle up against.

Before you ask why God killed a couple for telling a lie, ask, "Why didn't God kill me, when I lied for the first time!" All God did was to treat them according to their sins. When we did wrong for the first time and didn't get struck by lightning, we then concluded that God didn't see or didn't care about what we did, and with that, became more bold in our sin. Yet, all that happened was that God extended His mercy toward you and me, that we might have a time of grace to repent.

If we caught a revelation of what God is really like, we would fall flat on our faces in terror. Just take an objective look at some of His natural laws. If you break electrical or gravitational laws, the consequences are fearful, but they are merely a weak shadow of the eternal moral Law of God. My words cannot express what God is like, but His Law gives us some insight into His holy nature. The Law reveals utter holiness, supreme righteousness, and absolute truth. God has a violent passion for justice. What has your understanding of God been like? Do you tremble at the very thought of His power and holiness? Have you seen Him in the light of Holy Scripture, or have you made up a god to suit yourself? If that is the case, you are guilty of idolatry. The sentence for idolatry under the Law is death; and according to Scripture no idolater will enter the Kingdom of Heaven. Tomorrow, we will continue to look at each of the Commandments of God's Law.

QUOTE FOR TODAY: When a child pays attention to his parents, they're probably whispering.

* * *

FRIDAY

READING: Psalm 7

MEMORY VERSE: "God is a just judge, and God is angry at the wicked every day." Psalm 7:11

The third of God's Ten Commandments is, "You shall not take the name of the Lord your God in vain. For the Lord will not hold him guiltless who takes His name in vain." How many of us can say that we have always spoken God's name with due reverence? Listen to the way people use it as a  curse word to express disgust at something they don't like happening to them. If humanity is called to give an account of "every idle word," how much more when we have used God's name in such a way! Hitler's name was not despised enough to use in such a context.

The Fourth Commandment tells us, "Remember the Sabbath day, to keep it holy." I didn't keep this command for 22 years of my non-Christian life. Not for a second did I say, "God gave me life, what does He therefore require of me?" let alone set aside one day in seven to worship Him in spirit and in truth. Death is the sentence under the Law for Sabbath breaking.

The Fifth is, "Honor your father and mother." That means we are commanded to value them implicitly in a way that is pleasing in the sight of God. Have you *always* honored your parents in a way that's pleasing in God's sight? Have you always had a perfect attitude in all things towards them? Ask God to remind you of some of the sins of your youth. You may have forgotten them, God hasn't.

What is your most valuable possession? Isn't it your life? Your car, your eyes, your money, etc, are all useless if you are dead. So obviously, your life is the most precious thing you have. If you are in your right mind you will want to live a happy life and live a long one; yet you have God's promise that if you don't honor you parents you will have neither (Ephesians 6:1).

The Sixth is, "You shall not kill." But Jesus warned that if we get angry without cause we are in danger of judgment. If we hate our brother God calls us a murderer. We can violate the spirit of the Law by attitude and intent. Maybe you have the blood of abortion on your hands. Civil law may smile upon your crime -- God's Law calls you a murderer and the Sixth Commandment demands your death.

The Seventh is, "You shall not commit adultery." Who of us can say we are pure when Jesus said that we violate this command in spirit by lusting after a member of the opposite sex. He warned, "You have heard it said by them of old, 'You shall not commit adultery,' but I say to you, whoever looks upon a woman to lust after her, has committed adultery already with her in his heart." Until you find peace with God, you will be like a man who steals a T.V. set. He enjoys the programs, but deep within his heart is the knowledge that at any moment there could be a knock on the door and the law could bring him to justice.

Remember that He has seen every sin you've ever committed. He has seen the deepest thoughts and desires of your heart. Nothing is hid from His pure eyes. The day will come when you have to face that Law you have broken. The Scriptures say that the impure (those who are not pure in heart), the immoral (fornicators - those who have sex before marriage) and adulterers will not enter the Kingdom of God. Adultery carries the death penalty.

Tomorrow, we will continue to thoroughly go through the Law so that we might understand how sinful sin is, and how far we have fallen short of God's glory.

QUOTE FOR TODAY: Treat a dog with kindness, pet him often, feed him well, and he'll never leave you. The same principles usually work for husbands.

* * *

SATURDAY

READING: Psalms 8 & 9

MEMORY VERSE: "He shall judge the world in righteousness, and He shall administer judgment for the peoples in uprightness." Psalm 9:8

The Eighth Commandment is, "You shall not steal." Have you ever taken something that belonged to someone else? Then you are a thief. You cannot enter God's Kingdom. You may have stolen a book from a library, failed to pay a parking fine, or maybe you "borrowed" something and never returned it. God is not impressed with the *value* of what you stole. When you have stolen, you have sinned against God, you have violated His Law.

The Ninth Commandment is, "You shall not bear false witness." Have you ever told a fib, a "white" lie, a half truth, or an exaggeration? Then you have lied. How many lies do you have to tell to be a liar? Just the one. "*All* liars will have their part in the Lake of Fire" (Scripture cannot be broken). You and I might not think that deceitfulness is a serious sin, but God does.

The final nail in our coffin is, "You shall not covet." That means that we should not desire things that belong to others. Who of us can say we are innocent? All of us has sinned. As the Scriptures say, "There is none righteous, no, not one; There is none that understands, there is none that seeks after God." Just as with civil law, you don't have to break ten laws to be a law breaker, so the Bible warns, "Whosoever shall keep the whole Law, yet offend in one point, the same is guilty of all." The most blind of us will usually admit that man has glaring faults, we are forever transgressing against each other. But our transgressions are vertical, not horizontal; our real crimes are against God, not man. Without the Law, we look at sin from the standard of man; we have a distorted view. It takes the Law to give us insight to His standard, which is utter perfection. The Bible asks, "Who shall ascend the Hill of the Lord? -- He that has clean hands and a pure heart;" "Blessed are the pure in heart, for they shall see God;" "Be perfect as your Father in Heaven is perfect." How do you measure up? Are you perfect, pure, holy, just and good? Or have you caught a glimpse of what you must look like to God? The picture the Scriptures paint of us is not a nice one.

Over these last few days, as we have gone through the commandments, you may have suddenly seen that you never understood what sin is. If this is true, the worst thing you can do at this point in time is to say that you will change your lifestyle; that you will, from this day forward, live a good life. Let's say you were actually able to do that; from now on you will always not only *live* a good life but *think* pure thoughts. Who then is going to forgive your past sins? Can a judge let a murderer go free because he promises to live a good life from now on? No, he's in debt to justice. He must be punished. If you are not sure of your salvation, don't wait any longer, skip over to tomorrow's Words of Comfort and get things right with God.

QUOTE FOR TODAY: Gratitude to God should be as regular as our heartbeat.

* * *

SUNDAY

READING: Psalm 10

MEMORY VERSE: "The wicked in his proud countenance does not seek God." Psalm 10:4

The truth is, you and I have violated the Law a multitude of times. The Law, like a dam of eternal justice, has been cracked in numerous places and is towering over your head waiting to burst upon you. The Bible says, "the wrath of God" abides on you. Jesus warned that if the stone of a just and holy God falls on you, it will "grind you to powder." When you grind something to powder you do a thorough job. Every foul skeleton in the closet of every human heart will be brought out on the Day of Judgment.

The thought may have entered your mind that perhaps God will overlook your sins. Perhaps He, in His mercy, could just look the other way. If He does so then He is unjust. Think of it again in connection with civil law. Can a judge look the other way when a criminal is obviously guilty, and be true to what is right? Even if the judge feels sorry for the criminal he must stay true to the law; justice must be done. In the ten years between 1980 and 1990, in the United States alone, there were 60,000 murderers *who were never caught!* At least 60,000 murders were committed and the murderers got away totally free. No doubt the figure is higher as many "accidents" and "suicides" are actually murders in disguise. These are people who have raped, tortured and strangled helpless victims, cutting up their bodies or burning them without trace. Should God overlook their crimes on Judgment Day? Should He turn a blind eye? Should He compromise eternal justice? Or are you saying God should punish only the *serious* crimes? But your lying, stealing, adultery of the heart and rebellion *are* serious in His sight. No, the Bible says He will by no means clear the guilty. Who would like to see justice overlooked? Isn't it only the guilty?

Well, what is the punishment for sin? The Bible warns of everlasting damnation. It speaks of eternal Hell. Imagine if Hell was just a place of continual thirst. Have you ever had a thirst where you thought you'd die for lack of liquid? Or imagine if it were only a place of gnawing hunger? Or merely chronic toothache?

Have you ever been in pain where you felt you wanted to die? Have you ever felt the pain of a broken arm, leg or rib? The Scriptures warn that Hell will be a place of "weeping and gnashing of teeth;" a place of eternal torment; a place where death will not bring welcome relief to suffering; a place where God will withdraw every blessing He has showered upon sinful, rebellious, and ungrateful humanity; an abode where there will be absence of color, goodness, peace, beauty, love and laughter. A place of darkness, depression and despair, where murderers, rapists, those who have tortured, those who have stolen, lied, hated, been greedy, lustful, envious, jealous, blasphemous and rebellious to the command of God will dwell.

Hell is the place where sinful humanity will receive its just retribution for crimes against the Law of a Holy God. *How terrible sin must be in the sight of God to merit such just punishment!*

Tomorrow, we will continue to look at the subject of salvation. If you aren't sure you are saved, please take the time to read ahead to make your calling and election sure.

QUOTE FOR TODAY: Alcohol is the only enemy man

has succeeded in loving.

* * *

MONDAY

READING: Psalms 11 & 12

MEMORY VERSE: "For the Lord is righteous, He loves righteousness; His countenance beholds the upright." Psalm 11:7

Over the past few days we have been looking in depth at God's Law. The reason for this is to make sure you are saved. Imagine going through a devotional book, going to church, praying and hearing those most fearful words from the one you called "Lord," "I never knew you." If you are sure of your salvation, study this Biblical way to witness.

How's your conscience? Is it doing its duty? Is it accusing you of sin? Is it affirming the Ten Commandments to be right? If not, which of the Commandments do you say is unjust -- "You shall not steal," "You shall not bear false witness," "You shall not kill?" Perhaps you have committed adultery, or you have been longing for opportunity to. While no human being can point an accusing finger at you, the Ten Fingers of God's Holy Law stand as your accuser. You have been caught holding a smoking gun. The Law calls for your blood.

Under it, the penalty for adultery is death by stoning. I don't stand as your accuser, I hang my head in guilt as one who has been in your place. I, like every other red-blooded male, was an adulterer at heart. I could not, in good conscience, call for justice to take its course.

You are like the woman caught in the very act of adultery. The Ten Great Rocks of the Law are waiting to beat down upon you. My earnest prayer is that you will not attempt to justify yourself at all, but bow your head and agree with the Law and the impartial voice of your conscience, and  say, "Guilty! . . . what must I do?" In doing so, you are merely saying that God's testimony about humanity is true; that our hearts *are* deceitfully wicked to a point of not only being vile sinners but also being so deceitful that we will not even admit our own sins!

Like the woman, you have no other avenue to take. Your only hope is to fall at the feet of the Son of God. Ironically, there is only One human being who can call for justice to be done. And yet, He is the only one who can forgive sins. At His feet alone is the Law satisfied. If you humbly call on His name, you will hear, "Where are your accusers?" and be able to say, like the woman, "None Lord."

How could this be? Did God somehow compromise His justice through His Son. No! His justice was satisfied *through* His Son. What has happened is that the Law has stirred up the judge of conscience. The reason you could sin and not be concerned was because the judge had been wooed into a deep slumber. The thunderings of the Law awoke him and now he stands as your accuser. There is an air of indignation that he has been silenced for so long. He has come back from his slumber with a vengeance, and with each Commandment he says, "Guilty!" What then must you do to satisfy his charges? No monetary payment will stifle his accusation of liability; no prison sentence will silence his righteous charge. What is it that will free you from the torments of what the world calls a "guilty conscience?" There is only one thing that can do it -- the blood of Jesus Christ, " . . . How much more shall the blood of Christ, who through the eternal Spirit offered Himself without spot to God, *purge your conscience from dead works* to serve the Living God?" (italics added). In other words, anything you might try to do to save yourself from the consequences of sin is nothing but "dead works." Tomorrow, we will look at what God did to fulfil the demands of His Law.

QUOTE FOR TODAY: "Examine yourself in the light of God's holiness; you will find that God's Grace is as infinitely amazing as it is infinite." Christian Kingery

* * *

TUESDAY

READING: Psalms 13 & 14

MEMORY VERSE: "The fool has said in his heart, 'There is no God.'" Psalm 14:1

Remember, we have been studying God's Law to see

what sin actually is. We have done this so that you and I might, from that knowledge, find a place of genuine repentance, because if we are strangers to repentance we are not saved.

Let's look at the principles of civil law. Imagine you had broken the law. You are guilty of some terrible crime. You don't have two beans to rub together; *there's nothing you can do to redeem yourself.* Justice is about to take its course when someone you don't even know steps into the courtroom and pays the fine for you! If that happened, the demands of the law are totally satisfied by the one who paid your fine. You are free to go from the courtroom. *That's what God did for you and me.* When the Law utterly condemned us, Jesus Christ stepped into the courtroom and paid the fine for us by His own precious blood.

Words fail me to express His love which was demonstrated to us on that cross so long ago. When the Law called for our blood, Jesus gave His. When the justice of a holy God cried out for retribution, Jesus cried out on the cross in agony as He satisfied it by giving Himself on our behalf. The Law didn't just demand the death of the Son of God, it demanded the *suffering death of the perfect sinless Messiah.* Sin is such a serious thing in the sight of God, that the only thing which would satisfy His righteousness was the unspeakable suffering of a sinless sacrifice.

I heard the story of an African chief who got wind of a mutiny being planned in his tribe. In an effort to quash the revolt, he called the tribe together and said that anyone caught in rebellion would be given one hundred lashes, *without mercy*. A short time later, to the chief's dismay, he found that his own brother was at the bottom of the revolt. He was trying to overthrow him so that he could be head of the tribe. Everyone thought the chief would break his word. But being a just man, he had his brother tied to a tree. Then he had himself tied next to him, *and he took those 100 lashes across his own bare flesh*. In doing so, he not only kept his word, (justice was done) *but he also demonstrated his great love and forgiveness towards his brother*.

When God became flesh in the Messiah and suffered on the cross, He was not only showing that God was just, but He was also demonstrating the depth of His love and forgiveness towards you and me. Can you imagine how that brother felt as the chief took the punishment which was due to him? Can't you see how every lash of the whip would break his own rebellious heart. Can't you see tears well in his eyes and his face wince as he heard each lash of the whip? Is your own heart so hard that you can hear the nails being driven into the pure hands of the Son of God and not at all be moved by such love? Isn't there a cry in your own heart as you hear the agonies of the cross as the fury of a holy, just and righteous God was unleashed against Him . . . or have you a heart of stone? He suffered in our place, taking *our* punishment. May God make it real to you.

We are nearing the end of studying God's Law and His provision for our forgiveness. Tomorrow, we will draw this thought to a close. I realize that the past few Words of Comfort have been heavier than normal, but I couldn't think of anything worse than you enjoying what I have written and ending up in Hell. My greatest desire in life is not only to see sinners saved, but to see Christians raised up as laborers, totally equipped with the super sharp sickle of God's Law in hand.

QUOTE FOR TODAY: To err is human; to blame someone else is more human.

* * *

WEDNESDAY

READING: Psalms 15 & 16

MEMORY VERSE: "My heart also instructs me in the night season." Psalm 16:7

Imagine if I spent a great deal of effort trying to persuade you to put a parachute on. I did so by talking to you about the horrible consequences of ignoring the law of gravity.

What I was doing, was 'hanging you out of the plane by your ankles.' I was telling you what would happen if you hit the ground at the speed of 120 mph. Your eyes widened as I went into details. But, slowly it dawned on you that if you wanted to live you had better put the parachute on. You are convinced. It needs no more words from me. With trembling hand, you reach under your seat, *to find to your horror that there is no parachute!* Terror *really* gets a grip on you now as you think of the horrific death you have to face at any moment. Suddenly, you are awakened from your living nightmare by a kindly voice. Another passenger you have never seen before, is holding a parachute out for you to take. You reach out and take it in your trembling hands. Words can't express your gratitude. An unspeakable joy fills your heart as you realize that you don't have to die. The thought as to where the stranger got the parachute hardly enters your mind.

After the jump, you find that all the passengers have lived . . . *all but one.* It's only then you realize that the stranger gave you his own parachute *and went to his death so that you could live.*

That is what Jesus Christ did for you. He gave His life that you might be saved. A complete Stranger, Someone you didn't even know, did that for you. His was a willing, terrible, substitutionary death.

What you must do, if you have never done it before, is to truly obey the command of God to repent and put your trust totally and singularly in Jesus Christ. Your alternative is to have the full fury of God's Law unleashed against you on Judgment Day. You have no other option - *unless you repent, you shall perish.* There is no purgatory, no second chance, no other name, no other hope, no other way for you to be saved. Pray a prayer like this from your heart: "Dear God, I have violated your Law. I have broken your Commandments. I have sinned against You and You only.

You have seen my every thought and deed. You saw the sins of my youth, and the unclean desires of my heart. I am truly sorry. I now understand how serious my transgressions have been. If justice was to be done, and all my sins uncovered on the Day of Judgment, I know I would be guilty and justly end up in Hell. Words cannot express my gratitude for the substitutionary death of the Lord Jesus Christ. I may not have a tear in my eye, but there is one in my heart. I *really* am sorry. From this day forward I will show my gratitude for your mercy by living a life that is pleasing in your sight. I will read your Word daily and obey what I read. In Jesus' name I pray, Amen."

QUOTE FOR TODAY: One thing worse than a quitter, is the man who is afraid to start.

* * *

Other books, tapes and tracts by Ray Comfort include:

**BOOKS
Hell's Best Kept Secret (Evangelism - the use of the Law in evangelism) - $5
The Mantle of the Harlot (Sequel to *Hell's Best Kept Secret*) - $8
Militant Evangelism (Principles for aggressive evangelism) - $4
Springboards For Budding Preachers - valuable "How-to's" for street preaching and personal witnessing - crammed with ear-gripping anecdotes - $5
My Friends Are Dying! (Gripping and true story about the famed and murderous, drug infested MacArthur Park, L.A.'s area of highest crime) - $4
You've Got To Be Choking (Humorous illustrated look at L.A.'s air, also packed full of fascinating statistics, quality quotes and anecdotes) - $4
Reaching the Drug User - Drug abuse (written pre-Law) - - educational $2
God Doesn't Believe In Atheists . . . Proof the Atheist Doesn't Exist - $8
Russia Will Attack Israel - Excellent for unsaved - $3

**TAPESETS
Words of Comfort Six tapes - 1/ How to bring your children to Christ using the Law, 2/ Scriptures for memorization for preaching the Law, 3/ A message for America, 4/ Zeal for the lost 5/ Questions and answers regarding the Law, 6/ Atheism - $20
Hell's Best Kept Secret (six tapes - Why use the Law, How to use the Law and four other tapes to set you on fire for God) - $20
Hell's Best Kept Secret (sixteen tapes - this series contains all the tapes of the six series plus 1/ How to witness

effectively, 2/ How to battle the fear of man, 3/ How to obtain zeal, 4/ The occult, 5/ Keys to revival, 6/ How to answer objections and much more) - $48

**VIDEOS
Ten "Cannons" of God's Law - $14.95
How To Get On Fire For God - $14.95

**TRACTS (Please add postage)
Comic tracts 10 cents each.
IQ Cards $3 per 100 (Six "F"s).
IQ Cards $3 per 100 (Paris In The Spring).
IQ Cards $3 per 100 (Math Test).
IQ Cards $3 per 100 (Life/death).
Penny with Ten Commandments pressed onto it $5 per 200.
Natural Enquiry News $4 per 100.
Million Dollar Tracts $1 per pack.
Mad as Hell $1.50 per 40.
Are You Good Enough To Go To Heaven? $1 per 20.

**BOOKLETS - 50 cents each
1/ How to Make Your Marriage Blossom,
2/ The Pit Of Hell,
3/ Freedom From Fear of The Future,
4/ What it Means to be a Christian.

EVANGELICAL ENVELOPES Legal size $3 per 40

T SHIRT - BREAK ONE . . . BREAK 'EM ALL - $13.95 ($1 postage)

STUDY ON THE TEN COMMANDMENTS - Twelve weeks $3.50 ($1 postage)

SLEIGHT-OF-HAND pack (with instructional video) $24.95 ($1 postage).

Single tapes $3 each
1. Hell's Best Kept Secret (90 mins) .
2. Words of Comfort (one hour personal message to the unsaved).
3. How to get on Fire for God.
4. God Doesn't Believe in Atheists.
5. Militant Evangelism.

Laminated Ten Commandments (on quality paper) $1.50 ($1 S/H)
Bumper sticker - $3 ... 30"x4" Jesus said, "Unless you repent, etc"
Bible coloring book -- sleight-of-hand (simple to do, and very effective) $8

CHECKS -- TO LIVING WATERS PUBLICATIONS, P.O. Box 1172, Bellflower, CA 90706 - (CA add tax)